CRITICAL PERSPECTIVES ON
US ENGAGEMENT IN THE MIDDLE EAST

ANALYZING THE ISSUES

CRITICAL PERSPECTIVES ON
US ENGAGEMENT
IN THE
MIDDLE EAST

Edited by Anne C. Cunningham

Enslow Publishing

101 W. 23rd Street
Suite 240
New York, NY 10011
USA

enslow.com

Published in 2017 by Enslow Publishing, LLC
101 W. 23rd Street, Suite 240, New York, NY 10011

Cataloging-in-Publication Data

Names: Cunningham, Anne C., editor.
Title: Critical perspectives on US engagement in the Middle East / edited by Anne
C. Cunningham.
Description: New York : Enslow Publishing, 2017. | Series: Analyzing the issues |
Includes bibliographical references and index.
Identifiers: ISBN 9780766081291 (library bound)
Subjects: LCSH: United States—Foreign relations—Middle East—Juvenile litera-
ture. | Middle East—Foreign relations—United States—Juvenile literature.
Classification: LCC DS63.2.U5 C746 2017 | DDC 327.56073—dc23

Printed in the United States of America

To Our Readers: We have done our best to make sure all website addresses in this
book were active and appropriate when we went to press. However, the author and
the publisher have no control over and assume no liability for the material available
on those websites or on any websites they may link to. Any comments or suggestions
can be sent by e-mail to customerservice@enslow.com.

Excerpts and articles have been reproduced with the permission of the copyright
holders.

Photo Credits: Cover, Rawpixel.com/Shutterstock.com (meeting), Thaiview/
Shutterstock.com (background, pp. 6–7 background), gbreezy/Shutterstock.com
(magnifying glass on spine); p. 6 Ghornstern/Shutterstock.com (header design
element, chapter start background throughout book.

CONTENTS

INTRODUCTION

Peace in the Middle East seems an increasingly impossible endeavor. If recent American interventions have contributed to making this grim state of affairs worse, what should our role in the Middle East become? If past and present military operations have yielded a power vacuum now filled by opportunistic extremists, can we rectify this? Is it possible for America to protect its core interests without being drawn further into expensive wars that are unpopular politically? When it comes to the Middle East, the US would like it both ways: we wish to fully safeguard our national interests, just without any proportionate commitment of "blood and treasure." Will air strikes and high hopes alone do the job?

Among the many crucial questions pertaining to US engagement in the Middle East, this dilemma of waning American credibility and influence in the region coinciding with rising extremism and instability provides focus for many of the articles contained in the pages to follow. As one might expect, no easy answers are forthcoming. Nonetheless, a critical examination of recent history and geopolitical events will help us assess the options as they stand, and forge a more effective set of policy tools and objectives. Even if we agreed on such goals, mustering the resolve to follow through on them would challenge a twenty-first America more concerned with nation building at home.

The Middle East comprises over five million square miles of Asia Minor and North Africa. It has been a cauldron for ethnic and religious conflict, violent territorial squabbles, and generalized chaos for much of the twentieth century. In large part, this unrest can be traced back to the Zionist project from which the state of Israel sprung. The Zionist movement, backed by the US and former British Empire, created a modern nation-state for the Jewish people. After more than a century of European anti-Semitism, culminating with the horrific events of Nazi Germany, the idea of a Jewish homeland understandably gained much traction. That the Jewish state was established in territory occupied for generations by Palestinians was treated as a mere inconvenience. To counter the justified resentments and frustrations of this displaced, marginal population, Israel has leaned heavily on militarism—with the full support of the United States at every turn. In return, the US has gained a stalwart ally in an area where friends are in short supply.

This "special relationship" with Israel has been a cornerstone of US policy in the Middle East for many decades. However, there is evidence that it may be subject to some measured re-evaluation. The nuclear accord with Iran, Israel's "mortal enemy," represents a subtle realignment of US power. As we'll see, the deal has received mixed reviews.

Some see it as a welcome rapprochement with Iran, while others see it as too lenient. The latter hold Iran to be an untrustworthy partner, and feel that diplomacy threatens Israel's long-term security to an unwelcome degree.

Oil is another key US interest in the Middle East, but this too is changing. Until very recently, our domestic energy needs required a steady supply of oil from Gulf States such as Saudi Arabia. However, the United States is now experiencing an energy boom. Although fossil fuels from bituminous coal and shale gas come at a great environmental cost, they have provided the US with some energy independence. This has translated into some much needed leeway with foreign policy.

Finally, thwarting terrorism requires solid intelligence partners in the Middle East. Since 9/11, this has become a national obsession. Americans accept greater police powers and diminished civil liberties as a matter of course. Due to our failure to foster democracy in Iraq, and a brutal civil war in Syria, the Islamic State in Syria and Iraq, otherwise known as ISIS, has risen to worldwide notoriety as the preeminent terrorist organization and quasi-state. Though few disagree ISIS must be stopped, a ground invasion against ISIS is off the table—for good reason: experts agree such an act would likely backfire and help their already impressive recruitment efforts.

CHAPTER 1

WHAT THE EXPERTS SAY

A consensus exists among Middle East experts that the United States' long history of dominance in the region is over. However, views on whether or not this is a positive development diverge. Some see this as a rational recalibration to changing global realities and priorities; others regard it as the inevitable result of multiple ill-advised invasions and concomitant failures to foster democracy and stability in the region.

Despite brutal civil war in Syria, and the resulting humanitarian and refugee crisis, the Middle East is fading as a foreign policy priority. This is partially due to domestic methods of extraction such as hydraulic fracturing, or "fracking" that have decreased the United States' dependence on foreign oil. This newfound energy independence has given America more leeway to step back from regional conflicts that do not immediately threaten its interests. Is this pullback wise in the long term? Or will it invite more instability, aggression, and potential terrorist attacks on American soil? Such events would surely (and dangerously) reverse our tenuous restraint.

Still, the containment of ISIS remains a key US security objective, and the chaos in Syria and Iraq are seen as potential incubators for jihad. But as we've learned from Iraq and Libya, the US lacks the resources, ability, and political resolve to administer transitional governments effectively. So questions remain: is our gradual withdrawal from engagement in the Middle East really even a choice?

"HOW THE MIDEAST WAS LOST: NEITHER DICTATORSHIP NOR DEMOCRACY GUARANTEES AMERICA'S INTERESTS," BY TED GALEN CARPENTER, FROM *THE AMERICAN CONSERVATIVE*, JANUARY 2, 2012

The upheavals that engulfed the Middle East and North Africa in 2011 seemed to blindside the Obama administration and U.S. foreign-policy community. There was no indication at all that American officials anticipated the ouster of Tunisia's long-tenured pro-U.S. strongman Zine El Abidine Ben Ali. And just days before the size of the anti-government demonstrations in Cairo's Tahrir Square increased exponentially, Hillary Clinton's State Department opined that Egypt appeared stable and opposition forces would not topple Hosni Mubarak's three-decade dictatorship.

As the so-called Arab Spring gained momentum, the administration scrambled to catch up with events and turn the chaos to Washington's advantage. It has had only limited success in doing so, and developments of the past year have left the U.S. foreign-policy agenda in a tenuous position indeed. The Arab Spring arrived amid fading U.S. missions in Iraq and Afghanistan. By now it is apparent to all except the most enthusiastic imbibers of neoconservative Kool-Aid that the high hopes accompanying the 2003 invasion of Iraq were illusory. Post-Saddam Iraq will not become a pro-Western bastion, much less a model of democratic stability. Instead, under the increasingly autocratic rule of Prime Minister Nouri al-Maliki, Iraq is emerging as at best a quasi-democratic state with a pronounced pro-Iranian orientation. Clearly, that was not what Washington envisioned.

The looming outcome of the mission in Afghanistan is scarcely better. President Obama's decision to expand the number of troops deployed in that country has changed little: the Taliban remains strong, and the government of President Hamid Karzai is as corrupt and ineffectual as ever. Executing a gradual, reasonably dignified exit appears to be the only attainable U.S. goal.

Despite those setbacks, policy-makers are not about to abandon the effort to maintain an extensive U.S. presence, if not outright hegemony, in the heart of the Muslim world.

Once it became clear that Mubarak's rule was doomed, the Obama administration moved to salvage as much as possible of U.S. influence in the country. At the 11th hour, Washington urged its long-time client to leave peacefully and called on the Egyptian military to arrange a transition to elections and a new civilian government. The opinion elite in the United States remained divided on the wisdom of that approach. Hawkish right-wingers were vocal in condemning Obama's repudiation of a U.S. political ally, and they worried—with good reason—that Islamist forces, headed by the Muslim Brotherhood, were poised to gain dominance after Mubarak's ouster. The results of the first round of elections in early December confirmed that the Brotherhood's political arm, the Freedom and Justice Party, and the even more hardline Salafis bloc, can rout moderate and secular factions, with Islamists taking better than 60 percent of the votes for the People's Assembly, the lower house of parliament.

So even as Obama administration officials called on the army to act as midwife to Egyptian democracy, they worked assiduously to strengthen Washington's own ties to the military hierarchy. Whatever the administration's motives, the post-Mubarak power structure in Egypt began to look a lot like the old regime, sans Mubarak himself, with the military retaining real power. That may well be the way U.S. leaders like it.

A democratic Egyptian government with significant authority would not likely be pro-U.S., and it most certainly would not be friendly to Israel. But Washington is playing a risky game if it assumes that a friendly autocratic system has staying power, given the extent of public discontent in Egypt—as evidenced by another round of anti-military demonstrations in Tahrir Square on the eve of the December elections.

The Obama administration's strategy of trying to get in front of the tide of anti-regime populism was more evident in Libya. U.S. leaders quickly condemned the efforts of Libyan dictator Muammar Gaddafi to suppress the growing rebellion against his four-decade rule. It was easier for Washington to take that stance since, in contrast to Mubarak, Gaddafi was never a friend of the United States. Indeed, relations with his regime had been frigid until 2004 and 2005, when the mercurial dictator abandoned his quest for nuclear weapons and renounced support for terrorism. Even then, U.S.-Libyan relations remained tepid.

When it became apparent that rebel forces had a chance to oust Gaddafi, the Obama administration embraced the efforts of France, Britain, and other NATO members to assist the insurgency. Rather than openly advocate using military force for political reasons, though, the United States and its allies spun the fiction that a humanitarian intervention was needed to save the lives of Libyan civilians. With Russia and China willing to hold their noses and go along with that fiction, the UN Security Council approved military action. U.S. and NATO forces promptly launched air strikes and cruise-missile attacks, giving the rebels de facto air superiority.

Proponents see the Libya mission as a model for future U.S. interventions in the Middle East, North Africa, and elsewhere. It confined military action to air and naval support with no "boots on the ground"—the deployment of ground forces that would risk Western casualties and resulting political controversies. This was not really a new strategy; it was a reversion to the model that the Clinton administration used in the Balkan wars of the 1990s, an approach that relied on bombing largely helpless targets from high altitudes.

The Obama administration saw the Libyan mission as a potential model in another way. It was a strategy of "leading from behind"—providing crucial U.S. firepower and logistical support but pushing European allies to take the lead. U.S. officials and outside strategists dedicated to preserving U.S. dominance in the Arab world saw that approach as having the potential to achieve policy results without incurring the high costs and bitter domestic divisions that another massive Iraq-style intervention would inevitably generate.

As 2011 drew to a close, the administration was also taking a harder line toward the government of Syrian President Bashar Assad, and a Libyan-style military venture has become more than a remote possibility. As in the intervention against Gaddafi, advocates of using force to take out Assad cite the very real brutality of his crackdown on anti-regime demonstrators. Indeed, that line of argument has more validity than it did in the case of Libya. By December, Assad's security forces had killed an estimated 4,000 people since the uprising began, compared to just a few hundred deaths at the time of NATO's intervention against Gaddafi.

Not surprisingly, the United States has taken a far more pro-active stance against dictatorial regimes that were hostile to Washington than those considered friends—however corrupt and authoritarian those friends might be. American condemnation of the dictator of Yemen, Ali Abdullah Saleh, was noticeably milder than the denunciations of Gaddafi, Assad, and the clerical regime in Iran. And Washington's criticism of the Saudi-backed monarchy in Bahrain barely reached the level of perfunctory.

Reasons for the double standard were not hard to find. The Saleh government has been most helpful in assisting U.S. efforts to root out al-Qaeda cells in Yemen. And Bahrain is the homeport of the U.S. Fifth Fleet, which is the linchpin of the American naval presence in the Persian Gulf. American leaders are willing to risk charges of inconsistency—and even rank hypocrisy—to continue backing regimes that provide such crucial support for U.S. policy in the region, even if those regimes are both brutal and corrupt.

How Muslim populations react to Washington's double standard, though, is another matter. De facto U.S. support of Saleh, for example, did not save his regime—he has conceded to step down in February. And the Obama administration's conveniently selective stance regarding democracy and human rights in Muslim countries certainly has done nothing to refurbish America's tattered image with aggrieved populations.

The tumultuous developments of 2011 had one common feature: they portend a far more precarious military and political situation for the United States throughout the swath of territory from Morocco to the Pakistan-India border. American policymakers are working frantically to prevent a series of setbacks from becoming a geopolitical rout.

One objective is to preserve access to key countries—and key bases—for the U.S. military. Once it became apparent, for example, that there would be no long-term "residual" deployment of 20,000 to 30,000 U.S. troops in Iraq after 2011, Washington explored ways to beef up its military presence in Kuwait. The theory is that troops, planes, and ships located in that kingdom could be used to police hot spots elsewhere in the Middle East and Persian

Gulf. That same objective has made U.S. officials even more desperate to retain the U.S. naval base in Bahrain. But it is a fragile strategy. At the moment, the Kuwaiti ruling family seems secure in power, but then, so did other Arab regimes that quickly melted down during the Arab Spring. Bahrain is an even frailer candidate for a U.S. military bastion. Despite massive support from Riyadh, the repressive Sunni-dominated regime is ripe for overthrow by an Iranian-backed Shi'ite revolution. That could happen quite suddenly and put the future of the headquarters of the U.S. Fifth Fleet in doubt.

The uncertainty of continued military access to Kuwait, Bahrain, and other Gulf states means that Washington is coming to rely more and more on Saudi Arabia as its principal political and military ally in the Islamic world—especially as the United States adopts a more aggressive policy toward Iran, since there is a diminishing roster of regional partners for such a venture. Iraq is not going to be a reliable U.S. ally; indeed, the Shi'ite-led government in Baghdad would more likely tilt toward its co-religionists in Tehran in a U.S.-Iran fight. The turmoil in Egypt largely removes that option. And the chilling of relations between Washington and its NATO ally Turkey confirms that the U.S. can no longer count on that country to help implement its policy objectives in the Middle East.

These dynamics mean that Washington's military leverage in the region is less secure than it has been in many decades. And its political-diplomatic position is in even greater jeopardy. The landslide triumph of Islamist factions in Egypt's parliamentary elections is a sign that the Arab Spring may produce a host of unfriendly regimes. The earlier balloting in Tunisia also saw an Islamist party, albeit a somewhat moderate one, become the leading faction in that country's parliament. And one of the first actions of the National Transitional Council in Libya following Gaddafi's ouster was to declare Sharia law.

For decades, the foundation of Washington's policy throughout North Africa, the Middle East, and Southwest Asia relied on partnerships with friendly secular autocrats. That foundation is now crumbling, as one by one America's dubious security partners lose their grip on power. In response, U.S. leaders are pursuing a two-track strategy. One track is to try to prop up tottering regimes in key countries. The effort to preserve the Egyptian military's dominant role in that country and the U.S.-Saudi partnership to shore up Bahrain's royal family are examples of this. The other track is to portray the United States as supportive of the aspirations of downtrodden populations as symbolized by the Arab Spring. We see that approach in evidence with respect to U.S. policy in Libya and the ongoing effort to undermine the Assad regime.

Neither is working well. The friendly autocracies are finding it increasingly difficult to hold onto power, regardless of U.S. support. Indeed, Washington's great nightmare is that the most crucial remaining authoritarian partner, the Saudi royal family, might lose its grip. While that does not appear to be an immediate danger, it is a scenario that cannot be ruled out. The emergence of an anti-American regime in Riyadh would put all of Washington's major policy goals—protecting the oil flow, containing and undermining Iran, and supporting Israel's status and power—in dire straits.

Although the old foundation of partnership with autocrats is not doing well, the newer approach of backing reform isn't faring any better. Given its record, the United States has little credibility with Muslim populations as a champion of freedom and democracy. Indeed, U.S. policy-makers seem to assume that those populations have a collective case of amnesia about Washington's support for corrupt tyrants throughout the decades since World War II.

American foreign policy is adrift in a sea of increasingly hostile countries in North Africa, the Middle East, and Southwest Asia. The eastern anchor of American strategy, Pakistan, has already become such an unreliable partner in the war against radical Islamists in neighboring Afghanistan that some U.S. policy experts now regard Islamabad as an adversary rather than an ally. Afghanistan itself is a corrupt, ineptly governed mess with few prospects for stability-much less pro-Western stability—in the foreseeable future.

Farther west, the United States confronts the growing power of Iran; a new Iraq that, while nominally democratic, is also under mounting Iranian influence; and a Saudi Arabia that feels under siege and has little confidence in Washington's staying power. The United States can no longer count on Turkey. Under the Justice and Development Party of Prime Minister Erdogan, Ankara shows more pronounced Islamist tendencies and pursues an increasingly independent foreign policy.

Egypt, an ally for more than three decades, is now a less reliable partner—even if the military manages to keep the Muslim Brotherhood and the Salafis bloc from gaining decisive power. Libya seems more likely to be a fractious, pro-Islamist state than a secular democratic friend, despite NATO's sizable military and economic investment.

All this suggests that the era of U.S. hegemony in that part of the world is entering its twilight. But instead of adjusting to that change gracefully and adopting a lower political and military profile, the U.S. policy elite is inclined to dig in its heels and try to preserve a rapidly eroding position. That strategy is unlikely to work, and the oversized U.S. presence—especially the abrasive military presence—may well contribute to even greater turmoil and anti-American sentiment in the coming years.

1. The US policy goals identified by the author include "protecting the oil flow, containing and undermining Iran, and supporting Israel's status and power." Do you think revision of these policy goals is possible, or advisable? Why or why not?

2. Do you agree with the author's recommendation that the US adopt a lower political and military profile? What are the potential dangers of this approach?

"A VIOLENT SORTING OUT: MIDDLE EAST EXPERT JOSHUA LANDIS," BY RICHARD A. KAUFFMAN, FROM *THE CHRISTIAN CENTURY*, APRIL 30, 2015

JOSHUA M. LANDIS, associate professor at the University of Oklahoma and director of its Center for Middle East Studies, has served as a consultant to the State Department on Middle East issues. He is president of the Syrian Studies Association and runs the blog Syria Comment.

How did you become an expert on Syria, of all places?

I lived in Beirut and in Saudi Arabia for the first ten years of my life. My father worked for Citibank. After college I got a teaching job rather serendipitously in Lebanon in 1979, when Lebanon was in the middle of a civil war. I started learning Arabic and trying to figure out why the Lebanese were shooting each other. Two years later I got a Fulbright scholarship to the University of Damascus. I was there in 1982 when the Muslim Brotherhood took over the third-largest city in Syria. The regime smashed it, killing perhaps 20,000 people. Then I pursued Middle Eastern studies at Harvard and Princeton and wrote about Syria.

You saw early on the issues that were shaping Syria and Lebanon.

Right. And the civil war that I witnessed in Lebanon had similarities to what is going on today in Syria in that it was a sectarian struggle. All the regimes in the Levant area of the Middle East were run by religious minorities: Lebanon by the Maronites, Iraq by the Sunnis, Syria by the Alawites. You could even say that the Jews were a minority in Palestine that turned themselves into a majority.

Autocratic rule by a minority sets up a very unstable situation?

Yes, it is unstable. We've been seeing over the past 30 years the popular demand to get rid of these minority regimes. In Lebanon it took a 15-year civil war to do it.

In Iraq, Saddam Hussein was powerful enough not to be overthrown, despite many attempts, until the United States invaded and threw the Sunnis—who were 20 percent of the country—to the bottom of society and catapulted the Shi'ites—the 60 percent majority—to the top. That unleashed an unholy sectarian war.

How has Syrian president Bashar Hafez al-Assad been able to stay in power so long?

In large measure because he's been preparing for this sort of uprising for years. He placed Alawites, the Islamic sect he belongs to, in the top security positions in the military and in the intelligence agency so that they would not abandon him in a crisis. By contrast, the military in Egypt abandoned Mubarak and in Tunisia they abandoned Ben Ali. All through the Arab Spring countries the militaries turned against their dictators—but not in Syria, because the Alawite minority understood that they would be swept away were the

president to fall. They also have strong allies in Iran
and Russia and support from other minorities.

Some Christians even support the Assad regime.

Christians make up perhaps 5 percent of Syria's population. That figure used to be more like 14 percent, after
World War II. And there are the Druze, the Ismailis, and
the Kurds. But the Arab Sunnis are 70 percent of the population, by far the majority. There are quite a few Sunnis
who support the regime, oddly enough, because over 40
years many people worked for the regime or are impli-
cated in its rule. If the opposition were to take power,
many of the Assad supporters would lose their jobs and
probably their property as well.

What interests do Western powers have in Syria?

Historically, very little. Certainly the United States has had
limited interests. We've imposed sanctions on the country
since the 1970s and have almost no trade with it. Our main
interest is to not allow the chaos and violence in Syria to
bring down friendly regimes in the neighborhood. And, of
course, more recently our interest is in curbing ISIS and
radicalism in the region.

What can be done?

President Obama has made the assessment that it would be
damaging to the United States to try to organize a full-scale
occupation of Syria to disarm the radicals and construct a
new government—the sort of thing we attempted in Iraq (and

didn't attempt in Libya). His aim is to pursue a very narrow policy of counterterrorism, which some Americans argue we're good at. We can listen to the terrorists' phone calls, track them, and keep them in databases. If they come to the West trying to kill Americans, we'll kill them first. The president thinks this is a much less expensive and more doable policy than trying to somehow fix Syria and sort out the ethnic hostilities, defuse Islamism, and construct a liberal government along the lines the West would like.

The president has spoken of degrading and ultimately destroying ISIS. Is that feasible?

I think the degrading is going on. Destroying ISIS is not feasible—not with the policies that are now being pursued. President Bush wanted to destroy Islamic extremism and was willing to spend trillions of dollars to do it in Afghanistan and Iraq with an occupation. He believed that effort would lead to power sharing and the emergence of democratic governments that would have a domino effect in the Middle East—democracies breaking out all over. That didn't work out. The United States spent a lot of money on the effort. It managed to put the Shi'ites in power in Iraq, so we were partly successful. But that hasn't brought liberalism to the Middle East, and it hasn't been an antidote to extremist Islamism. In fact, it has inflamed Islamism. Al-Qaeda is now well ensconced in Iraq. ISIS, a breakaway group from al-Qaeda, now controls one-third of Iraq and one-third of Syria. That is a direct byproduct of the U.S. occupation of Iraq. Fifteen of the top 20 officers under Caliph al-Baghdadi, the leader of ISIS, are former members of the Baathist Party in Iraq who were thrown out of power when the United States overthrew Saddam, and most of them spent long periods of time in American prisons.

Are you saying there's a revenge factor for these ISIS leaders?

They don't like America, but their main goal is to rule the Middle East and not to be ruled by the Shiites who were put in power by the United States in Iraq and who pushed the Baathists out of government in the country.

You have said elsewhere that military intervention by the United States in Syria would be a disaster. Why?

Theoretically, if you had NATO and international support, lots of money, and a willingness to stay for 20 or 30 years, you could rearrange Syrian society, rebuild its economy, provide people with education, and build a middle class and a new government. Obviously, the United States is not going to do that because we have had almost no interest in Syria. Throwing arms into the area in the hope that somehow good people are going to end up on top is a very risky policy and one that's leading to the breakdown of Syrian society and the growth of jihadism.

Is there anything that the United States can do or should do?

It should spend a lot more money on helping and educating the refugees. The United States needs to set a clear agenda for the regional powers that are supporting the radicals. Turkey, for example, has been allowing al-Qaeda and ISIS to move back and forth across its territory. And Arabs in the

Persian Gulf states have been pouring money into all kinds of jihadist groups.

You've talked in other places about a great "sorting out" happening in the Middle East. What do you mean?

What's going on in Lebanon, Israel, Syria, Iraq—the entire Levant—is a nation-building process. It's similar to what happened at the end of World War I when major empires were destroyed. World War I in many ways was an empire-destroying war—it dismantled the Russian empire, the German empire, the Austro-Hungarian empire, and the Ottoman empire. The 1919 Paris Peace Conference at the end of the war drew borders rather haphazardly. The result was a series of multiethnic, multisectarian countries stretching from Poland to Palestine. These new borders and new nation states jumbled different peoples together, and many of these people did not want to live with each other. This led to great tensions and the emergence of fascist and supernationalist movements. With the rise of Hitler all this exploded.

With World War II there was a great sorting out in Europe. Poland was 64 percent Polish before the war, but by the end of the war it was almost 100 percent Polish. Six million Jews had already been killed in this region. Thirteen million Germans were ethnically cleansed from Central Europe in just two years, between 1945 and 1947. A third of Czechoslovakia was made up of minorities, but by the end of the war the minorities were all gone. That's the pattern in Ukraine and Hungary, too. In Yugoslavia, Tito acted as a little emperor, and he held his mosaic together with coercion, but as soon as he was swept away the nation exploded into a very brutal ethnic war and was chopped into seven countries.

The same sorting out of ethnic groups has been and is happening in the Middle East. Half of Israeli citizens are Jews who came from the Middle East, where every major capital had a large Jewish neighborhood before World War I or before World War II. These Jews were caught between the hammer and anvil of Arab nationalism and Zionism. And almost every one of those Jewish neighborhoods is gone. There are a few Jews left in Morocco, Istanbul, and Iran, but the Jews in Yemen, Syria, Iraq, Lebanon, and Egypt are gone.

Christians are leaving too.

There aren't many Palestinian Christians left, and most Iraqi Christians have left. About 60,000 Christians in Iraq's Mosul were kicked out in one day with the ISIS conquest. The Yazidis have been enslaved or forced to convert or have fled. And Syria's largest city, Aleppo, in the north, was well over 20 percent Christian after World War I. Many Armenians had fled there from Turkey; Anatolia was 20 percent Christian before World War I. By the end of the Turkish revolution, which ended in 1922, Ataturk kicked the Greek army out and in the process ethnically cleansed the country of Christians. The Armenians had already been ethnically cleansed, so those 20 percent are gone. In Turkey less than 1 percent are Christians today, and Christians have not been allowed to build churches. This sorting out simplifies the life of these countries. (The United States had its sorting-out process too—it got rid of Native Americans and other challengers.)

So the outlook is bleak for minority groups?

Space can be created for minority groups. Space could have been created for a Palestinian state in half of Israel, for example, but the Palestinians are increasingly being pushed out. It takes a commitment from the international community to save these minorities, and the international community ultimately doesn't care.

If you were asked to advise the Obama administration on Syria, what would you say?

I would say: try to help Syria's neighbors settle as many Syrians as they can, and help them get educated so they don't become a cauldron of future terrorists and freedom fighters.

Some Westerners think the Islamic world needs to go through a Reformation or Enlightenment of sorts. What do you think?

The dominant ideologies in the region are still absolutist and stem from the Qur'an, providing a religious justification for action. The region resembles Europe in the early modern period after the Reformation. Europe was embroiled in religious wars after the rise of Protestantism—from the late 1400s until the Treaty of Westphalia in 1648. Finally Catholics agreed that Protestant princes could be

Protestant, that Protestants could build churches and worship, and that they weren't an abomination. In a way the Enlightenment has begun in the Middle East. Look at the big debate in Iran today: President Rouhani says that he should be the true leader because elections brought him to power. And he wants to make a deal with the Americans. But Supreme Leader Khamenei says no, I'm the supreme leader, and God has empowered me, and this is a divine republic, an Islamic country. Does authority stem from God or from the people? That debate is going on everywhere in the Middle East. And Shi'ites and Sunnis have to find an accommodation, a way both can exist under their version of a "separation of church and state."

So the fact that this debate is going on provides some hope?

It does provide hope. How do you encourage the debate? It requires education, opportunity, a solid middle class. Putting sanctions on countries is counterproductive. We had sanctions on Syria for decades. The estimates are that it reduced the GDP by 2 percent a year. We thought that Syria would then do a pirouette, leave Iran's sphere of influence, make peace with Israel, and love America because of a desire to get out from under the sanctions. It didn't lead to that; it led to civil war and a breakdown. We put sanctions on Sudan, we put sanctions on Libya, we put sanctions on many countries, and it's not led to the outcomes we wanted because we've impoverished people. And we're doing it to Iran today. It may lead to a good outcome, but it could break the country.

How important are the youthful demographics in many of these countries?

Social scientists who study age have concluded that a revolution has a more than 50 percent chance of leading to a democratic transition if the median age of the population is 30 years old or older. In countries like Syria and Iraq, however, the median age is 21 years old. In Egypt it's 24; in Gaza and Yemen it's 18.

So the younger the population, the more likely that extremists will prevail?

Yes, because the younger people want radical change, and they're willing to risk a lot because they don't have a lot invested in the society. It makes more sense to go through a revolution if you're young, because even if it takes 15 years to sort things out, you'll be only 35 then and still have a future. But if you're 50 and experience a revolution, and it only gets sorted out after 20 years, you're dead. It's hard for us to imagine what it's like to have a revolution in a country where the median age is 21.

Where do you see Israel fitting into this major sorting out in the Middle East?

Israel has gone through a sorting out, although not completely. The Jews were one-third of the population in 1948 when Israel got independence and the British left. They've made themselves into a very powerful majority. The Palestinians have largely lost, and it doesn't look like a two-state solution is in the offing. It looks like the Palestinians are going to live in some form of subjugation for a long time. This sorting out is long and bloody. It's been long and bloody in Israel, and it's going to be long and bloody in much of the neighborhood. In Lebanon, the sorting is not over. Christians still retain 50 percent of all seats in Parliament-Sunnis and Shi'ites each get one-fourth of the seats—yet Christians are less than a third of the population. There are over a million Sunni Syrian refugees in Lebanon, a country of 4 million people. That has completely thrown off the sectarian balance. Once those Syrian refugees get their feet on the ground and a generation has been brought up in Lebanon who feel Lebanese and not Syrian, they're not going to stand for the political arrangement.

Should the United States allow many more Syrian refugees to come here than what we have so far?

The entire world has to do more to try to alleviate these pressures. You can't just hold people in a tent. In the 19th century those people would have been able to leave and go to the New World. Today that's not the case; nobody wants immigrants. The world is filled up; we have good borders with fences, and we're building one with Mexico today to keep out the press of humanity from the south. Look at Gaza: it's a ward of the entire West Bank, it's a ward of the international community. It doesn't produce anywhere near the wealth that it consumes. You don't want to set up refugee camps that become permanent cauldrons of injustice.

European countries haven't done a great job of assimilating immigrants, have they?

Well, they've taken on a lot of Muslims very quickly. In Sweden, for example, 20 percent of the population was born outside the country. In America the figure is only 13 or 14 percent.

European nations are trying to figure out how to be multicultural societies after being rather homogenous. It's difficult to do. Every time the United States got close to having a 20 percent immigrant population—in the 1920s and a few other times—anti-immigrant parties have grown fairly strong. It's not an easy process.

> 1. Why does Joshua Landis state that the US goal to completely destroy ISIS is "not feasible"?

"DECONSTRUCTING THE SYRIA NIGHTMARE," BY MICHAEL E. O'HANLON, FROM *THE NATIONAL INTEREST*, OCTOBER 22, 2015

FORGET PEACE IN SYRIA. THE INTERNATIONAL COMMUNITY MUST INSTEAD WORK TO CREATE POCKETS OF MORE VIABLE SECURITY AND GOVERNANCE OVER TIME.

U.S. policy towards Syria since the Arab Spring uprisings of 2011 has been a litany of miscalculation, frustration and tragedy. The ascendance of the Islamic State in Iraq and the Levant (ISIL) as the major element of the opposition to the Bashar al-Assad regime may not amount to an imminent threat to American security; indeed, to date very few Americans have died at the hands of ISIL or its affiliates.

But ISIL's rise does place at much greater risk the security of Iraq, the future of Syria itself and the stability of Lebanon and Jordan. It could jeopardize the safety of American citizens as well, given the possibility of attacks by Westerners returning from the Syrian jihad or "lone wolves" inspired by ISIL propaganda. Massacres on a par with the Charlie Hebdo tragedy, or worse, could easily occur in the United States. The potency of the al-Nusra organization, Al Qaeda's loyal affiliate, within the Syrian opposition is also of considerable concern.

This is not a situation that requires an invasion of Syria by tens of thousands of Western troops. But nor is it a situation that can be allowed somehow to burn out on its own. Even if the Assad regime soon falls to combined opposition forces, the problem will hardly be solved, since ISIL might then be in a position to dominate an entire country rather than just half. An ISIL advance westward would put the 10 to 15 percent of the population made up of "apostate" Alawites, as well as the 10 percent of the population that is Christian (according to prewar tallies), at severe risk of massacre. Upheaval in Syria would intensify, having already displaced half the country's population and ended a quarter of a million lives. All of this would further validate ISIL's apocalyptic narrative of a caliphate beginning in Syria—a narrative that, even if it has no chance of being realized, could aid the group in its already-impressive recruiting efforts, which are currently bringing about one thousand new fighters a month to the battlefield. This pace is probably adequate to replenish the loss rate from U.S.-led air strikes, estimated by one U.S. official to have killed ten thousand ISIL fighters. Indeed, the U.S. government's upperbound estimate of some thirty thousand ISIL fighters has not changed for months despite the air campaign.

What's needed to end the carnage is a radically new approach: working toward a confederal Syria. Put even more starkly, the only credible path forward is a plan that in effect deconstructs Syria, especially in the short term. A comprehensive, national-level solution is too hard even to specify at this stage, much less achieve. Instead, the international community should work hard, and devote substantial resources, to create pockets of more viable security and governance within Syria over time. With initial footholds in place, the strategy could develop further into a type of "ink-spot" campaign that sought to join the various local initiatives into a broader and more integrated effort.

This approach builds on the ideas of classic counterinsurgency efforts but has a much different application. In this case, of course, the United States and foreign partners are taking the side of the insurgents rather than the government, and the goal is not to defeat the insurgency but to support and empower it.

This strategy might produce only a partial success, liberating parts of the country and then settling into stalemate. But that should not be seen as failure, even if it happens. One possibility is two or three safe zones in more remote parts of the country, backed up by perhaps one thousand American military personnel and other countries' special-operations forces in each (with an implied annual cost of perhaps several billion dollars), rather than a snowballing and successful nationwide campaign. Generalizing the strategy from, say, the Kurdish areas of the country in the northeast (where a "lite" version of such an approach is now being attempted by Ankara and Washington), to the heavily populated and intermixed population belt from Idlib and Aleppo through Homs and Hama to Damascus could be very difficult. It would be substantially more dangerous, and also much more logistically challenging. It would be important that Washington not precommit to comprehensive regime change on any particular time horizon, since the number of available "moderate" partner forces may not prove adequate to that task, even once recruiting and training begin within the safe zones.

In fairness to the Obama administration, a realistic and comprehensive plan for Syria has always seemed elusive, without even factoring in self-imposed U.S. political constraints. And now, American "allies" in the war together constitute perhaps the fifth-strongest fighting force in the country, after Assad's own military, ISIL, al-Nusra and even Hezbollah. Some of these so-called allies may not be so moderate, or dependable, after all. Kurdish fighters in Syria have had some success, and are now integral to a plan Ankara and Washington have developed to establish a safe zone in northern Syria that will greatly complicate ISIL's ability to connect logistically with the outside world. But the ability of the Kurds to liberate any territory further south is unclear, and Turkey's willingness to go along with any such escalation of the Kurdish role is also in doubt.

The woes go on. The central peace process appears to be in tatters. Moderate forces are not currently strong enough to achieve a significant governing role through any plausible negotiation outcome. Any willingness by Assad to defect as part of an integrated plan to produce a new power-sharing government (perhaps backstopped by an international peacekeeping force) would likely be seen as evidence of weakness by his enemies. It would probably fail to produce a durable and stable outcome. An actual large-scale U.S. military intervention is off the table, in light of what the nearly decade-long effort in Iraq produced; not even the most hawkish candidates in the GOP field for president in 2016 are calling for such an approach. Development of a new Syrian army of tens of thousands, able to take on Assad as well as ISIL, may be conceptually appealing. But it seems hugely ambitious in a situation where the United States has failed to train even a few thousand moderate fighters a year, and where there are few individuals who could provide political or military leadership of an integrated Syrian opposition. An integrated army may be the right long-term plan, but it is probably not a realistic goal with which to begin.

Were Assad foolish enough to challenge these zones, even if he somehow forced the withdrawal of the outside special-operations forces, he would be likely to lose his airpower in ensuing retaliatory strikes by outside forces, depriving his military of one of its few advantages over ISIL. Deconflicting U.S./allied efforts to attack ISIL with the expanding Russian activities in the country would, however, be important.

With this approach, given the direct American and other allied assistance that would be provided, one could be confident that sanctuary sites would never again have to face the prospect of rule by either Assad or ISIL. They would also constitute areas where humanitarian relief could be supplied, schools could be reopened and larger opposition forces could be recruited, trained and based, un agencies and NGOs would help in the effort to the extent they were willing and able, focusing on health, education and basic economic recovery. Governing councils would be formed, more likely by appointment than election, to help international agencies make decisions on key matters relevant to rudimentary governance. Regardless of details, relief could certainly then be provided more effectively than today.

At least one such area should adjoin Jordan and another Turkey, and these should be created in cooperation with Amman and Ankara. These locations would allow secure transportation lines for humanitarian as well as military supplies. They would also provide bases from which to attack ISIL in its strongholds, a mission that Western forces could carry out in conjunction with local allies. The ultimate endgame for these zones would not have to be determined in advance. The interim goal would be a deconstructed Syria; the ultimate one could be some form of a confederal Syria, with several highly autonomous zones. One of those zones might be for Alawites, perhaps partly protected by Russian forces. But none of the zones could be for ISIL, al-Nusra or Assad and his inner circle.

At some point, the emergent confederation would likely require support from an international peacekeeping force, once it could be somehow codified by negotiation. The United States should be willing to commit to being part of a force, since without it, it is dubious that the conflict's various parties will have confidence in the stability of any settlement. The challenge of creating governance structures that protect the rights of Syria's various communities would be especially acute in the intermixed central population belt of the country. But in the short term, the ambitions of this strategy would be limited—they would be, simply, to make individual zones defensible and governable, to help provide relief for populations within them and to train and equip more recruits so that the zones could be stabilized and then gradually expanded.

As safe zones were created, over time some would eventually coalesce. For example, once appropriate understandings were reached with Turkey, a single Kurdish zone would make sense. Major sectors in the south near the Jordanian border, and in the north near Idlib and Aleppo, could be logical. Over time, if and when feasible, zones near some of the central cities such as Hama and Homs could be envisioned, though the logistical challenges and the safety challenges for Western forces (and the difficulty of collaborating safely with any Russian forces) could be greater in those cases. Prudence would have to be the watchword. In some cases, even the various members of the so-called moderate opposition might come into conflict with each other; outside parties might have to threaten to withhold support of various types to discourage such behavior.

The plan would be directed in part against Assad. But it would not have the explicit military goal of overthrowing him, at least not in the near term. American forces could concentrate on supporting opposition units fighting ISIL. Still, this plan would probably have the effect of gradually reducing the territory that Assad governs, since it would train many more opposition fighters and would not try to prevent them from liberating areas of the country currently controlled by the central government. If Assad then delayed too long in accepting a deal for exile, he could inevitably face direct dangers to his rule and even his person. The plan would still seek his removal, but over a gradual time period that allowed for a negotiated exit—with stronger moderate opposition groups part of the negotiation than is the case today—if Assad were smart enough to avail himself of the opportunity. In the short term, however, the current tacit understanding with Assad, whereby he chooses not to challenge Western airpower in Syria when it is used against ISIL, ideally would continue.

The opposition would need to accept that a peace deal that includes post-Assad Alawite elements remained Washington's goal—and if they wished economic and other help down the road for rebuilding a new Syrian state, they would have to tolerate some influence for the United States as well as other key outside players. This approach, while not ideal for many elements of the opposition who surely seek more systematic revenge against Assad and his cronies, could nonetheless provide a more workable basis for making common cause than is the case today, since it would in fact ultimately aim for an end to Assad's rule. For these reasons, whether they fully endorsed it or not, America's main regional allies in the effort—Turkey, Jordan, Saudi Arabia and the Gulf states—would likely welcome such an approach since it would move significantly in the direction they have advocated. Moreover, it would be more credible than previous American strategies, stated or implied, because its means would better match ends.

This strategy might soften Iran and Russia's opposition to the broader approach as well—perhaps reducing their inclination to escalate support for Assad and also possibly even enlisting them in an eventual negotiated deal about Syria's ultimate future and associated peace-enforcement operations. Indeed, the strategy strikes a balance in its approach to Iran and Russia. It would grant neither a major role. But it would seek to mitigate the risks of escalating rivalry with them by holding out political hope and the prospect of an autonomous region for Alawites (even those previously associated with the Assad regime, as long as they were not from Assad's inner circle). This approach may appeal even more to Moscow and Tehran if Assad continues to suffer battlefield setbacks. Damascus and Moscow would be much more likely to support a confederal Syria to the extent they believe that the alternative has become the complete overthrow of Assad and his government, the elimination of meaningful Alawite influence in a future government or, in a best case, civil war of indefinite duration.

An ultimate settlement could include outright partition of the country if necessary. However, partition would not solve the question of how to address the mixed cities of the country's center belt. As such, while it should not be taken off the table, it would hardly represent a panacea.

Should Assad fall, the essence of this strategy would still apply, but in a modified way. Moderate insurgents would still need strongholds from which to build up capacity to challenge ISIL (the presumed main winner in such a defeat of Assad).

Ideally, the U.S. Congress would explicitly support this strategy, but existing authorities and funds are adequate to start now. Ideally, the UN Security Council would endorse the approach, too—including the near-term idea of providing relief (without Assad's blessing) in some safe zones, and the longer-term goal of deploying a peace-implementation force to support an eventual peace deal. But again, given the emergency situation, the security stakes and the UN's interest in the notions of the responsibility to protect and the prevention of genocide, existing authorities are sufficient to embark on this strategy.

The basic logic of this ink-spot and regional strategy is not radical. Nor is it original or unique to Syria. In effect, variants of it have guided Western powers in Bosnia, in Afghanistan in the 1980s and since 1993 in Somalia. The last case is particularly relevant. Somalia, while a site of tragedy for U.S. forces in 1993, has since shown some signs of hopefulness. The Puntland and Somaliland in the north are largely self-governing and autonomous. Similar types of zones would be the interim goal for Syria as well.

We must be honest with ourselves: the interim period, including some type of American engagement in the war effort, could last a long time. For a country weary of long wars in the Middle East, this would constitute an on-the-ground role in yet another. That said, it is worth bearing in mind that while the Afghanistan war today continues to consume American resources and cost some American casualties, it is not a major source of domestic political acrimony within the United States. Perhaps Americans are more patient with long military operations than is often argued. That is especially the case if the strategy that the operations are designed to serve is responsive to a real security threat, and if it is at least moderately successful in its implementation.

There would of course be risks associated with this strategy. The most glaring would be the possibility of American casualties—either through "green on blue" insider attacks of the type that have taken dozens of American lives in Afghanistan, or through ISIL or regime elements overrunning a safe zone in which American forces are located. This is a significant risk, to be sure, and one that would have to be carefully managed, as noted above, by careful selection of where the safe zones are to be. It would also require deployment of American quick-reaction forces in the area, in more locations than they currently are found today, to improve the odds of coming to the aid of such U.S. forces in a timely fashion if their positions are brought into danger. In these ways, the operation in Syria would resemble the beginning phases of the Afghanistan campaign in 2001 and 2002, in which modest numbers of U.S. forces worked closely with the Northern Alliance and then the fledgling Afghan government, participating in raids and occasionally suffering casualties. Casualties could also be expected in any future peace-implementation mission, as spoilers use suicide bombs and other weapons to attack outside forces.

It is worth noting that two other types of risks associated with this strategy would be no greater, and in most ways probably less, than under current policy. First, there is the matter of U.S. prestige. Some would argue that by declaring itself committed to a change in battlefield dynamics, the United States would lose more prestige if in fact that proved more difficult to achieve than anticipated. But this risk must be measured against the real blow to American credibility that has already resulted from four years of an ineffective policy. Moreover, even partial success would help liberate and improve the lots of millions of Syrians who are now living under ISIL, Assad or anarchy.

Washington is already at war with ISIL—not only as a matter of formal policy but also in the ongoing bombing campaign underway in Iraq and Syria today, ISIL has already demonstrated its lack of restraint in its dealings with the United States in the 2014 beheadings of American hostages within its reach. Its social-media outlets are already trying to encourage lone-wolf attacks against the United States and its civilian population today, ISIL is currently encouraged by a sense of sanctuary and a sense of military momentum. Making Western attacks against ISIL more effective seems just as likely to put the group on the defensive as to occasion new attacks. In acting more aggressively to stabilize Syria and defeat ISIL, the Obama administration would not be plunging America into a new conflict. Instead, it would be recognizing that it is already engaged in one.

1. Do you think this "ink blot" strategy of protected zones can work in Syria? If so, do you think Americans can and should lead this process?

2. Do you think this approach underestimates the immediate danger and likelihood violence will escalate in the region?

CHAPTER 2

WHAT THE GOVERNMENT AND POLITICIANS SAY

Chapter Two begins with remarks prepared by Vice President (then Senator) Joe Biden, upon returning from his seventh trip to Iraq. As long as a decade ago, signs existed indicating that the Bush-led invasion of Iraq could prove disastrous. In the years since, this has only grown. Sectarian violence between the three major players in Iraq, the Shiite security forces, Kurdish minorities, and the Sunni insurgency has devolved into something resembling a civil war-torn failed state. Finding and training reliable US partner forces on the ground has proven immensely difficult. This is the vacuum into which ISIS has stepped, now controlling major cities in Iraq.

How do we deal with this threat? Secretary of State Ash Carter spells out a nine-point plan to counter ISIS. But given that many of his recommendations are common sense, and others are difficult to enact, it remains to be seen if these points will prove effective.

As Iraqi and Syrian conflicts have grown more intractable, the US has pivoted towards détente with Iran. In the last article of the chapter, Jonathan Broder takes a close look at the context into which John Kerry's nuclear accord with Iran sits. While many praise this as a needed step towards peace, others point to Iran's history as evidence this deal is a mere temporary fix, and one that will likely backfire.

"BREATHING ROOM: STEPPING BACK TO MOVE FORWARD IN IRAQ," BY JOSEPH R. BIDEN JR., FROM *THE NATIONAL INTEREST*, SEPTEMBER TO OCTOBER 2006

IN JULY, I made my seventh trip to Iraq. From military bases in Basra, Fallujah and Anbar province to Baghdad's Green Zone, I spent time with our diplomats and our generals, with Iraqi political leaders and with our troops. Even forty-eight hours on the ground, in a protective bubble, makes more vivid all that we have achieved—and all that we still must overcome. In Iraq, we confront two parallel realities. Our military and civilians are doing extraordinary work, under the most difficult conditions—and they are getting results. For example, the Iraqi army is much more capable than it was just a year ago, thanks to an increasingly effective U.S.-led training effort.

But for all our achievements, the larger reality is this: Iraq—and the success of America's mission there—remains prisoner to terrible and growing sectarian violence. Sectarian violence has trumped the insurgency and foreign terrorists as the main security threat in Iraq. In December 2005, Iraqis voted by the millions, but 90 percent cast their ballots along sectarian lines. Far from a democratic turning point, the elections reflected Iraq's deepening fault-lines. Since then, ethnic militias increasingly have become the law in large parts of Iraq. They have infiltrated the official security forces, especially the police. Meanwhile, Iraqis have less electricity, clean water, sewage treatment and oil than before the war. Iraq's government ministries are barely functional. Iraq looks closer to a failing state than an emerging democracy.

Understandably, the voices calling for an immediate withdrawal of American troops from Iraq are getting louder. Most Americans want to see our military personnel leave Iraq as quickly as possible. But it matters profoundly what we leave behind. A precipitous withdrawal risks trading a dictator for chaos, including a failed state careening towards a civil war that could embroil the rest of the region. Unfortunately, President Bush does not have a strategy for victory in Iraq. His strategy is to prevent defeat. It is not enough to say our plan is to stand down as Iraqis stand up. What we need is a plan to get Iraqis to stand together.

Ten years ago, Bosnia was drowning in ethnic cleansing and facing its demise as a unified state. After much hesitation, the United States stepped in with the Dayton Accords to keep the country whole by, ironically, separating it into ethnic federations. We even allowed Bosnians, Croats and Serbs to retain separate armies. With the help of U.S. troops and others, Bosnians have lived a decade in peace. Now, they are strengthening their common central government, and disbanding their separate armies. To be sure, it has been a fragile peace, but one that looks mighty appealing when compared with the carnage in Iraq.

In Bosnia, we navigated between two extremes: an ultra-realist approach of permanent partition and an idealist approach of immediately forcing people back together who needed some time apart. Instead, a pragmatic and progressive policy maintained Bosnia as a single country but gave each community breathing room and time to reconcile. The Bush Administration, despite its profound strategic misjudgments, has a similar opportunity in Iraq, but only if it is willing to fundamentally change course. "Staying the course" sounds strong, but it isn't smart when you've been steering by a fundamentally faulty compass. We have to break the cycle of mistake accumulating upon mistake, acknowledging uncomfortable facts on the ground and adjusting our strategy accordingly. Together with Les Gelb, president emeritus of the Council on Foreign Relations, I proposed such a change of course with a five-point plan premised on the notion that a political settlement must be found that gives all three major communities in Iraq Kurds, Shi'a and Sunnis—a stake in the future in Iraq, incentives to pursue their interests peacefully and space for a cooling off period—similar to the one in Bosnia.

The first element of this plan is to establish three largely autonomous regions with a strong—but limited—

central government in Baghdad. This central government would be responsible for common interests like border defense, foreign policy, oil production and revenues. The regional governments—Kurd, Sunni and Shi'a—would be responsible for managing their own affairs, from education to family law to economic policy.

The United States need not impose this solution. Iraq already has a federalist structure. The new constitution provides for Iraq's 18 provinces to join together in like-minded regions. In the Iraqi constitution, not unlike our own Articles of Confederation, local law trumps the national.

Some will ask whether this plan will lead to sectarian cleansing. The answer is that it's already happening. Dozens of dead bodies turn up daily in Baghdad. Since the al-Askariya mosque bombing in Samarra in February 2006, some 200,000 Iraqis have fled their homes for fear of sectarian reprisal. All told, more than 1.3 million Iraqis are internally displaced, and two million more have left the country since 2003, many of them the very middle-class professionals Iraq needs to build a functioning state and society. The Bush Administration's inability to establish security in Iraq's cities has been particularly damaging to our post-reconstruction efforts. In this plan, Baghdad would become a federal zone, while densely populated areas with mixed populations would receive both multi-sectarian and international police protection. The goal—as in Bosnia—is to prevent further sectarian cleansing and to re-establish order.

Let's be clear: a comprehensive political settlement won't end the Sunni insurgency, but it will give the Sunni political leadership a far greater stake in its own affairs.

This should serve to marginalize the insurgents and to make the insurgency more manageable. Similarly, while decentralization won't end the militia problem overnight, it is the best way to begin rolling it back. Militias have so heavily infiltrated the security forces that our training program is effectively making them better killers. Prime Minister Maliki's National Reconciliation program recognizes these problems. But without addressing the underlying security vacuum that gave rise to these militias in the first place, the new Iraqi government will be unlikely to succeed in reining them in where the American-led Coalition Provisional Authority has failed. The Iraqi constitution already provides for regional security forces; the regions can therefore become magnets for the militias, integrating them into local forces. Eventually, as individuals, not, as at present, as sectarian units, they can join a national force.

Increasingly, each community will support federalism, if only as a last resort. The Shi'a know that they can dominate the government, but they can't defeat a Sunni insurrection. The primary demand of the Kurds is to consolidate the autonomy they've built up over the past 15 years, but to also preserve a united Iraq as protection against the Turks. Until recently, the Sunnis sought a strong central government because they believed they would retake power. Now, they are beginning to recognize that they won't and that the greatest danger to their interests is a highly centralized, Shi'a-run state that gives them short shrift on resources and rights, and enforces the law with militia.

But for the Sunnis to fully accept federalism, they must be given assurances that their region would be economically viable. Virtually all of Iraq's exploited oil reserves are in the Kurdish and Shi'a area. So the second part of the plan would guarantee the Sunnis a fair share of Iraq's present and future oil reserves, proportionate to their size of Iraq's population. The central government would set national oil policy and distribute the revenues, which would reinforce each community's interest in keeping Iraq intact. International supervision would ensure transparency. Iraq's oil wealth would be the glue that keeps the country together.

Such an arrangement requires amending the constitution, a process the U.S. ambassador to Iraq, Zalmay Khalilzad, worked into the constitution just before it was proposed to the Iraqi people in a referendum, in order to secure Sunni political participation. The Shi'a and Kurds should support such an amendment because it would be in their economic self-interest. Petroleum experts agree that the Iraqi oil industry will attract more desperately needed foreign capital if it is run as a unified whole. Shi'a and Kurds will get a slightly smaller piece of a much larger pie. That's a better deal than they would get by going it alone, which will not attract the needed investment. At the same time, guaranteeing Sunnis a piece of this pie will reduce the incentive of insurgents to attack the oil infrastructure. That would be good news for everyone.

The third element of the plan is to rejuvenate the American reconstruction program. The incompetence of the Bush Administration's reconstruction program makes more reconstruction money and a jobs program a hard sell. But both are necessary. The large number of angry young men without jobs is feeding the Shi'a militia, the

Sunni insurgency and criminal gangs. A new aid effort would have to be radically different than the old one. For example, instead of international mega-firms pocketing valuable contracts, spending a huge chunk of each one on security, and then falling short, Iraqis should be in the lead of small-scale projects that deliver quick results and generate local jobs. All future U.S. aid would be clearly and unambiguously tied to the protection of minority and women's rights. We should insist other donors set the same standard. Aid would be cut off in the face of a pattern of violations. President Bush is now silent on protecting minority and women's rights. If they are not upheld, there can be no hope for eventual democracy in Iraq.

The president also should insist that other countries make good on old commitments—to date, just $3.5 billion out of some $14 billion pledged by other countries has actually been delivered—and provide new ones. He should focus on the Gulf States. They have a tremendous stake in avoiding a civil war that becomes a regional war—bringing in Turkey, Iran, Syria either directly or through proxies and pitting Shi'a against Sunni. And they're enjoying windfall oil profits. They should step up and give back.

There will be no lasting peace in Iraq without the proactive support of the international community, particularly the country's neighbors. This is the fourth element of the plan—a regional security conference, convened by the United Nations, where Iraq's neighbors, including Iran, pledge to respect Iraq's borders and behave cooperatively. Iraq's neighbors have a strong interest in not seeing Iraq descend into a civil war that could engulf them. But they also might be tempted to interfere in its weakened affairs.

We should create an ongoing mechanism to keep them in line. For two years, I've called for a standing Contact Group, to include the major powers, that would engage the neighbors and enforce the commitments they make at the international conference. The recent outbreak of violence centered on Lebanon makes this admittedly more difficult, but arguably even more necessary if we are to achieve a lasting cease-fire based on a commitment to disarm Hizballah and extend the Lebanese government's control over the totality of its territory.

The political settlement envisaged here would reduce sectarian violence and provide each community with a cooling off period, giving us our best chance of getting our troops quickly—and safely—out of Iraq. The continued presence of 130,000 American troops risks creating a culture of dependence. It drains vital resources from the larger War on Terror, and it risks putting an intolerable strain on the all-volunteer armed forces. We cannot sustain this large a force in Iraq without sending troops back on fourth and fifth tours, extending deployments from twelve to 18 months, and fully mobilizing the Guard. That would do serious long-term damage to our military. Thus, as a fifth element of the plan, the president would direct U.S. military commanders to redeploy almost all U.S. forces from Iraq by 2008.

Phased redeployment is also necessary because while the Iraqi patience with military "occupation" is running out, we still have not reached the tipping point— Iraqis want us to leave, but not immediately. At the same time, the widespread perception in the Middle East that we intend to stay in Iraq and control its oil feeds the insurgency and provides a recruiting boon for Al-Qaeda. Our military leadership has publicly acknowledged as much. Thus, we need to make clear that we do not intend to stay in Iraq forever. To help address this problem, I proposed and the Senate recently approved an amendment to this year's Defense Authorization bill that prohibits the construction of permanent U.S. military bases in Iraq.

The goal, in short, is to reconcile the increasing pressure to leave with the need to ensure that we do not leave behind chaos. The political settlement I propose, coupled with a phased redeployment—with targets but no hard deadline, and subject to change if conditions required—can do just that.

Even in a best-case scenario, Iraq's violence will not disappear overnight. Therefore, the plan proposes maintaining a small residual force of perhaps 20,000 troops in northern Iraq, assuming the Kurds welcome our presence; in Kuwait, in the unlikely event they don't. The force could strike any concentration of terrorists, help keep Iraq's neighbors honest, and continue the training of its security forces. Some U.S. troops and police would also need to participate in a multinational peacekeeping force deployed to the major multisectarian cities, as in the Balkans. At present, securing the participation of many other countries in such a force is a non-starter. But a political settlement—and a regional conference and Contact Group to demonstrate international resolve—could change their calculus and willingness to participate.

One of the consistent criticisms advanced against this plan for Iraq is that it amounts to partition. The opposite is the case. Iraq is coming apart at the seams. It is on the verge of violently partitioning itself. Only a dramatic change of course will keep the country together. This plan—what might be seen as a "division within unity" approach—is consistent with Iraq's constitution and new unity government. It is also consistent with-and I believe necessary to—the goal of keeping Iraq unified within its existing borders, preserving America's interests and bringing most of our forces home.

More and more Americans are rightly frustrated that the debate on Iraq among policy-makers and politicians has ossified into a Hobson's choice between "staying the course" and "cutting and running." This plan offers a third way forward. Yes, it comes with its own risks. But to those who reject it out of hand as unrealistic or unattainable, my answer is simple: What is your alternative?

1. Do you agree with Biden's proposal? Has the increased sectarian violence invalidated his five-point plan? If so, what should we do now?

2. Looking back at the situation a decade ago, does the current unrest in Iraq seem inevitable? Are Biden's premises fundamentally flawed, or merely too little too late?

"STATEMENT ON U.S. POLICY AND STRATEGY IN THE MIDDLE EAST BEFORE THE HOUSE ARMED SERVICES COMMITTEE," BY ASHTON CARTER, FROM THE *US DEPARTMENT OF DEFENSE*, JUNE 17, 2015

AS DELIVERED BY SECRETARY OF DEFENSE ASH CARTER, WASHINGTON, D.C., WEDNESDAY, JUNE 17, 2015

Chairman Thornberry, Ranking Member Smith, all Members of the Committee: thank you for inviting me here today. Thank you also for keeping a wide-ranging and long-term perspective on the challenges and opportunities for America and its leadership around the world. Just a couple of weeks ago, I was in Singapore, Vietnam, and India, and next week I'll be in Germany, Estonia, and Belgium, for a NATO ministerial. I understand that your focus in this hearing is current developments in the Middle East, and I'd be happy to answer questions about anything else.

The Middle East, as the Chairman noted, is undergoing a period of great social and political turmoil with a number and variety of cross-cutting geopolitical developments. Our strategy in the region, America's strategy, is grounded in America's core national interests – that's the foundation – tailored to address specific circumstances in specific and various places – Iraq, Syria, Iran, and so forth. And it leverages American leadership with the efforts of coalition – of a coalition of allies and partners.

Our core interests, for example, drive our actions to prevent Iran from acquiring a nuclear weapon. Similarly, our core interests dictate that we not let up until we have destroyed ISIL and al-Qaeda-affiliated terrorists throughout the region that pose dangers to the homeland, to friends, and to allies. The past few weeks serve as a reminder to terrorists bent on harming the United States and our interests, whether they're in Libya, Syria, or Yemen, that we have the capability to reach out and strike them.

Meanwhile, the security of Israel will always be one of my top priorities - and the Chairman [of the Joint Chiefs of Staff] just returned from Israel this past weekend. And we'll continue to hone important security relationships with our partners in the Gulf, bolster their security, and ensure freedom of navigation there.

The pursuit of our nation's core interests in the region is a strategy based on tireless diplomacy backed by formidable military power and dedicated capacity building to buttress and leverage the contributions of others, and especially, as noted, those in the region themselves.

That's why we have 35,000 forces postured throughout the region, enabling us to strike ISIL and al-Qaeda terrorists and check Iranian malign influence.

That's why we're assuring Israel's continued qualitative military edge, and why we're working with our Gulf partners to make them more capable of defending themselves against external aggression.

That's why we're supporting Saudi Arabia in protecting its territory and people from Houthi attacks, and supporting international efforts to prevent Iranian shipments of lethal equipment from reaching Houthi and Saleh-affiliated forces in Yemen.

And that's why the United States is supporting efforts to pursue political settlements to crises throughout the region, from Yemen to Libya to Syria.

While I'm prepared for a range of questions related to DoD's role in the Middle East, I'd like to focus on the immediate issue that I understand the Committee is interested in – namely, the U.S.-led coalition's strategy to defeat ISIL.

ISIL presents a grave threat to our friends and allies in the Middle East; elsewhere around the world from Africa and Europe to parts of Asia because of its steady metastasis; and to our homeland because of its avowed intentions to strike and recruit in this country. ISIL must be – and will be – dealt a lasting defeat.

The strategy to degrade and ultimately defeat ISIL constructed by President Obama draws upon all the national security agencies of the U.S. government: intelligence, law enforcement, diplomacy, and others. The strategy and its associated military campaign also involve a global coalition, reflecting both the world-wide consensus on the need to counter this threat and the practical requirement for others to do their part. And the counter-ISIL strategy has nine – nine so-called lines of effort, reflecting the breadth of this challenge and the tools needed to combat it.

The first and most critical line of effort is the political one, which is led by the State Department. In Iraq, this involves building more effective, inclusive, and multi-sectarian governance. Each of the other lines of effort requires success in this line because it's the only way to create support among local forces – and local people – that support being necessary to make progress against extremism stick.

The next two lines of effort are interconnected – to deny ISIL safe haven, and to build partnership capacity in Iraq and Syria. Both are led by the Department of Defense, which, alongside coalition partners, is conducting a bombing campaign from the air, advising and assisting Iraqi security forces on the ground, and training and equipping trusted local forces.

I will address our military's current execution of these two lines of effort in a moment, but I want to under-score a crucial point about our campaign in Iraq and also Syria: it requires capable, motivated, legitimate, local ground forces to seize, clear, and hold terrain – that's the only way to ensure a truly lasting, enduring defeat of this movement.

The fourth line of effort is enhancing intelligence collection on ISIL, which is led by the National Counter-terrorism Center. The fifth line of effort, which is disrupting ISIL's finances – a vital task – is co-led by Treasury and State. Lines of effort six and seven, both co-led by State and the National Counterterrorism Center, are to counter ISIL's messaging and to disrupt the flow of foreign fighters to and from ISIL, both of which are critical in today's connected and networked world. The eighth line of effort, providing humanitarian support to those displaced by or vulnerable to ISIL, is led by State. And finally, the Department of Homeland Security and the FBI are working together to protect the homeland – the ninth so-called line of effort – by disrupting terrorist threats here. The effective execution of all nine of these lines of effort by the United States and its coalition partners is plainly necessary to ensure overall success.

Let me turn to the execution of DoD's two lines of effort, beginning with the U.S.-led campaign of air strikes against ISIL in Iraq and Syria. This effort has produced some clear results – in limiting ISIL's freedom of movement, constraining its ability to reinforce its fighters, and impeding its command and control. It has enabled some key achievements for local forces – including the very recent success of anti-ISIL forces who took the key town of Tal Abyad. The strikes are also buying critical time and space to carry out DoD's second line of effort, which is developing the capacity and capabilities of legitimate local ground forces.

The ground campaign is a work in progress. The Iraqi Security Forces were severely degraded after Mosul fell last June, when four divisions dissolved. The combination of disunity, deserters, and so-called ghost soldiers – who are paid on the books but don't show up or don't exist – had greatly diminished their capacity.

However, understanding these challenges does not change reality – ISIL's lasting defeat still requires local forces to fight and prevail on the ground. We can and will continue to develop and enable such local forces, because we know from experience that putting U.S. combat troops on the ground as a substitute for local forces will not produce enduring results. That's why DoD seeks to bolter – bolster Iraq's security forces to be capable of winning back, and then defending and holding the ISIL-controlled portions of the Iraqi state.

What we saw in Ramadi last month was deeply disappointing, and illustrated the importance of a capable and motivated Iraqi ground force. In the days that followed, all of us on the President's national security team, at his direction, took another hard look at our campaign across all nine lines of effort. At DoD, I convened my team before, during, and after my trip to the Asia-Pacific and Indian Ocean region to examine our execution of DoD's lines of effort, and prepare options for the President if his approval was required for any enhancements we identified.

In our meetings at both the White House and the Pentagon, we determined that while we have the right strategic framework, execution of the campaign can and should be strengthened, especially on the ground.

We determined that our training efforts could be enhanced and thus are now focusing on increasing participation in and throughput of our training efforts, working closely with the Iraqi government and stressing the focus on drawing in Sunni forces, which as noted are underrepresented in the Iraqi Security Forces today. We also determined that our equipping of the Iraqi Security Forces had proceeded too slowly. This process was delayed by bureaucracy in Baghdad, but also in Washington. That's why we're now expediting delivery of essential equipment and material, like anti-tank capabilities and counter-IED equipment, to the Iraqi Security Forces – including Kurdish and Sunni tribal forces.

We also determined that we could enable Iraqi Security Forces with more tailored advice and assistance, including with critical outreach to Sunni communities. That's why, on advice from Chairman Dempsey and General Austin, and at my recommendation, last week President Obama authorized the deployment of 450 personnel to Iraq's Taqqadum military base in Anbar Province to establish an additional site where we could advise and assist the Iraqi Security Forces.

Situated between Ramadi and Fallujah, Taqqadum is a key location for engaging Sunni tribes, and Prime Minister Abadi, Iraqi military officials, and Sunni leaders have all committed to using Taqqadum to reinvigorate and expedite the recruitment of Sunni fighters. Our forces will also provide much-needed operational advice and planning support to the Iraqi Security Forces' Anbar Operations Center, which is also located at Taqqadum. We expect that this move will open a new dimension in our and Iraq's efforts to recruit Sunnis into the fight, and to help the Iraqis coordinate and plan the critical effort to roll back ISIL in Anbar province.

And Secretary Kerry and I have agreed to begin a process of continually assessing execution of our campaign, starting with improving coordination across our respective lines of effort.

Execution, however, is a two-way street, and our training efforts in Iraq have thus far been slowed by a lack of trainees – we simply haven't received enough recruits. Of the 24,000 Iraqi Security Forces we had originally envisioned training at our four sites by this fall, we've only received enough recruits to be able to train about 7,000, in addition to 2,000 Counterterrorism Service personnel. As I've told Iraqi leaders, while the United States is open to supporting Iraq more than we already are, we must see a greater commitment from all parts of the Iraqi government.

There are positive signs. I've met with Prime Minister Abadi, Iraqi Kurdistan Regional President Barzani, and just last week with Speaker Jabouri of Iraq's parliament. They all fully understand the need to empower more localized, multi-sectarian Iraqi security forces and address persistent organizational and leadership failures.

And because a sovereign, multi-sectarian Iraq is more likely to ensure a lasting defeat of ISIL, the United States must continue working with and through the Iraqi government in all our actions – including our support for Kurdish and Sunni tribal forces. Our efforts need to reinforce inclusivity and multi-sectarianism, not fuel a reversal to sectarianism which would make the lasting defeat of ISIL harder, not easier.

The situation in Syria is even more complex, because of the lack of a legitimate government partner, and many competing forces there. Regardless, we will continue striking ISIL in Syria with the long reach of our airstrikes and operators. We will continue working with Syria's neighbors to impede the flow of foreign fighters into and out of Syria and Iraq. Our train-and-equip mission in Syria has been challenging, but the requirement for a capable and motivated counter-ISIL ground force there also means we must persist in our efforts.

In conclusion, I believe that success in this campaign can and must be assured. It will take time, and require consistent effort on everyone's part – the entire U.S. government, our entire international coalition, and most importantly, the Iraqi and Syrian peoples. Together, and with your support – including your support for America's troops and their families, for which I, and they, are ever grateful – we will achieve ISIL's lasting defeat.

I'd be happy to address your questions.

1. The Secretary of Defense's claim that "putting U.S. combat troops on the ground as a substitute for local forces will not produce enduring results" is basically now taken as an article of faith by all who agree with Obama's general approach to the region—but does this conclusion strike you as fully accurate, or merely politically and economically expedient for America? Explain your answer.

2. Carter fails to address how the US will entice Sunni tribes to side with Iraqi Security Forces rather than ISIS (here referred to as ISIL). Do you see the questionable legitimacy of Iraqi government as a potential problem?

"GAMBLING ON IRAN: THE NUCLEAR DEAL AND THE LEGACY OF JOHN KERRY," BY JONATHAN BRODER, FROM *NEWSWEEK*, AUGUST 21, 2015

At the end of May, during a pause in the Iran nuclear talks in Switzerland, Secretary of State John Kerry was riding his bike around Lake Geneva when he accidentally hit a curb and crashed. This was no ordinary accident.

Kerry's thigh bone broke close to his hip, which doctors had previously replaced. Such a painful injury might have required another 71-year-old to lie in bed for months. But in just four weeks, the tireless Kerry bounced back. Hobbling on crutches in his signature blue suit and pink pastel tie, he flew to Vienna at the end of June for the final round of talks with Iran. In marathon sessions that often lasted into the early hours, Kerry worked through his pain and hammered out what could prove to be one of the world's most significant nonproliferation treaties.

The deal, which severely restricts Iran's nuclear program for at least 15 years in return for easing sanctions, represents both a physical and professional comeback for Kerry, who first tried and failed last year to etch his name into diplomatic history by brokering an Israeli-Palestinian peace accord. But with his victory in Vienna—and the likelihood that the Iran deal will survive a September challenge in Congress—Kerry is poised to provide Barack Obama with his signature foreign policy achievement. Some observers even predict the deal puts Kerry in line for a Nobel Peace Prize.

"It's an enormous diplomatic accomplishment. There's no question that it has profoundly changed the status quo," P. J. Crowley, a veteran of President Bill Clinton's National Security Council and Hillary Clinton's State Department, tells *Newsweek*. "There was a major issue that had the potential to lead to a military confrontation, and through effective diplomacy, he sidelined it. This is exactly what you expect a diplomat to do." Kerry, he adds, has now established a valuable channel of communication with Iran that can be used for future diplomatic efforts.

Already, the former Massachusetts senator is talking optimistically about working with the Iranians to address the conflicts in Syria, Iraq and Yemen. "I know that a Middle East that is on fire is going to be more manageable with this [nuclear] deal, and [it] opens more potential for us to be able to try to deal with those fires," Kerry told the Council on Foreign Relations on July 28. Aides say he's also eager to give Israeli-Palestinian peace talks another try.

But former officials and experts caution that the diplomatic challenges facing Kerry in the Middle East in the wake of the agreement promise to be even more difficult than the Iran negotiations. David Rothkopf, the CEO and editor of the FP Group, which publishes Foreign Policy magazine, and a supporter of the nuclear agreement, argues the deal has strengthened Iran considerably, first by lifting its pariah status and opening the way for European countries, along with China and Russia, to once again do business with Tehran. The agreement will also add some $150 billion in unfrozen assets to Iran's coffers, providing it with the means to fund its regional proxies, including embattled Syrian President Bashar Assad, Lebanon's political and militant group, Hezbollah, Shiite militias in Iraq and Houthi rebels in Yemen. And all this is happening as Iran's Sunni Arab neighbors have been weakened by wars, revolutions and the declining price of oil. "Everybody involved—the Iranians, the Europeans, the Chinese, the Russians, the Israelis, the Saudis—[is] looking at the post-deal lay of the land in the Middle East as significantly different from what it was before the deal," says Rothkopf.

As Obama implements the nuclear accord, Rothkopf warns he also will need to find ways to offset Iran's increased strength and influence in a region under-going enormous upheaval. "U.S. national interests are not advanced simply by one deal," he says. "They're advanced in the context of everything that's going on."

Washington's first moves will involve strengthening the defenses of its allies in the region. The Pentagon is already fielding a Saudi request for 600 Patriot missiles at a cost of $5 billion—the first of several expected arms deals with Arab allies in the Persian Gulf. The administration is also expected to boost military sales to Israel beyond the $3 billion in weapons it already receives annually. But Middle East experts say such weapons sales won't be enough to manage the broad power shifts in the region. In the years to come, the biggest challenge in the Middle East will be rebuilding war-devastated Syria, Iraq, Yemen and Libya. If that doesn't happen, these places will become breeding grounds for violent extremists, much like those areas of Iraq and Syria now under the control of Islamic State, or ISIS. Longer-term solutions will be necessary, these experts say, and they will require Iran's cooperation.

There are signs that Washington and Tehran are already moving in that direction. Until now, the Obama administration refused to allow Iran any role in a U.S.-proposed political solution for Syria. (The U.S. wants Assad and his top lieutenants to step down and a managed transition to a new government.) But in his July 15 news conference—just a day after the Iran nuclear deal was announced—Obama offered the Iranians a seat at the table. "I think that it's important for them to be part of that conversation," he said.

A solution to the Syrian problem also requires the participation of Russia, which supports Assad, as well as Turkey, Saudi Arabia and Qatar, which back the Syrian rebels. Some observers believe Russia could be convinced to abandon Assad, provided Moscow gets to maintain its naval base in Syria's Mediterranean port city of Tartus and its commercial arms relationship with the next government. Iran also might be persuaded to step back from Assad, but it would insist on maintaining its weapons pipeline through Damascus to Hezbollah, which threatens Israel's northern border. Kerry would be hard-pressed to overcome Israeli objections to such an arrangement. There are also concerns that Assad's departure could cause the government to collapse altogether, eliminating the prospect of a successor regime from within its ranks.

U.S. cooperation with Iran in the fight against ISIS predates the nuclear accord. Under a tacit alliance between Washington and Tehran, U.S. warplanes have been conducting airstrikes against ISIS positions for more than year now while Iran-backed Shiite militias have fought them on the ground. U.S. military officials say they provide air support only to Shiite militias that are under Baghdad's command, but in the fight in March for the city of Tikrit and in later battles, American warplanes ended up helping fighters under Iran's control. Closer coordination with the Shiite militias, however, could present Obama with political problems at home since U.S. military officials haven't forgotten that hundreds of American troops died at the hands of the Shiite fighters during the Iraq war.

In Yemen, the U.S. says it's providing logistical and intelligence support to a Saudi-led military campaign against Iran-backed Houthi rebels. But quietly, the administration is urging Riyadh to stop its offensive. In late May, Newsweek has learned, Anne Patterson, the assistant secretary of state for Near Eastern affairs, secretly met with senior Houthi officials in Oman. Shortly afterward, the Houthis released journalist Casey Coombs, one of several Americans the Houthis are believed to be holding, in return for additional U.S. pressure on the Saudis to halt their bombing campaign, Western diplomatic sources say.

Peter Feaver, a former official on President George W. Bush's National Security Council and a critic of the Iran deal, says the success of such diplomacy—and Kerry's place in the pantheon of great secretaries of state—will depend on whether he can make the agreement part of a larger strategy that realigns Iran according to U.S. national security interests. He's not optimistic. "It's a gamble that bets against history and that bets against Iran's pattern of behavior," he says. "And it's a gamble that is riskier than it needed to be because we could have had a better deal."

Defending the nuclear accord before Congress this week, Kerry recounted the moment of quiet reflection in Vienna's ornate Palais Coburg hotel after he and fellow diplomats from Iran and five major powers reached the nuclear agreement. French Foreign Minister Laurent Fabius noted that the date of the agreement was July 14—Bastille Day, which marks the beginning of the French revolution in 1789. Fabius then expressed confidence that the Iran deal would create another historical marker.

Maybe. But for now, most observers are reserving judgment. Aaron David Miller, who served as a Middle East adviser to both Democratic and Republican administrations, says the agreement remains "transactional" at this point, a business deal in which each party gets something from the other. In other words, Nobel Peace Prize or not, Kerry is likely to go through a lot more pain before the deal ever leads to a true detente between the U.S. and Iran.

1. The nuclear accord Kerry reached with Iran makes Iran significantly wealthier. Do you think this will embolden the country to flex muscle internationally, potentially threatening Israel? Or make Iran more akin to, and therefore friendlier with, secular, Western, capitalist nations?

2. Peter Feaver claims that the US-Iran nuclear deal is riskier than necessary. Do you agree? Why or why not?

CHAPTER 3

WHAT THE COURTS SAY

There exists a pernicious fiction that wars begin legally and above-board. According to this narrative, executive and legislative branches of government, adhering rigidly to constitutional guidelines, form a legitimate consensus regarding when and in what manner to engage a foreign adversary militarily.

Just as broken clocks are right twice a day, this has only been the case a few times in history. Still, legitimate declarations of war, and clear codes of conduct within war, however ideal, are not normative descriptions of how conflicts escalate in the twenty-first century. In practice, US military interventions appear an improvised patchwork of CIA-backed rebel groups, drone strikes of dubious legality, and other covert operations befitting our increasingly privatized military-industrial complex.

As one might expect from this picture, legal contests stemming from military actions are keeping the dockets full at US district, appeals, and Supreme courts, as well as military tribunals. Moreover, since the September 11 terrorist attacks, the president has been given a freer hand in directing military operations—a freedom some fear could backfire in the wrong hands.

At the beginning of this chapter, Jed Babbin advances a position asserting that former president Obama's drone strikes and other maneuverings exploited legal ambiguities and loopholes, but are still bad policy—and potentially dangerous. Conversely, David French argues that overly restrictive rules of engagement have put our troops lives in jeopardy.

"OBAMA'S DRONE WAR: IS IT LEGAL? IS IT CONSTITUTIONAL? AND IS IT THE RIGHT POLICY?" BY JED BABBIN, FROM *THE AMERICAN SPECTATOR*, MAY 2013

Back in the days when we had them, declarations of war were short, simple, and dear. By contrast, the "Authorization for the Use of Military Force" (from here on AUMF) cobbled together by Congress and signed by President Bush after 9/11 reads more like a generic threat addressed, "To whom it may concern." It authorizes the president "to use all necessary and appropriate force against those nations, organizations, or persons he determines planned, authorized, committed, or aided the terrorist attacks that occurred on September 11, 2001, or harbored such organizations or persons, in order to prevent any future acts of international terrorism against the United States by such nations, organizations, or persons."

This authorization, aiming America's military might at whomever the president deemed responsible for the attacks, was unprecedented. It created a vague legal framework for a war against no specified enemy over whom we could achieve victory, a war whose aims were so amorphous that it could continue forever. George Bush called this conflict a "global war on terror," but the left so ridiculed the phrase that even Bush gave up on the term. Twelve years later, after more than a decade of American troops in action, we're finally withdrawing from Afghanistan, just as we withdrew from Iraq. We have lost thousands of lives in an absurd Wilsonian pursuit of democracy in two nations where it is precluded by Islamic law.

President Obama's drone campaign is, in some ways, a limited version of Bush's global war on terror. (What else do you call it when the American military is fighting terrorists in places ranging from Afghanistan to Yemen, from Mali to the Philippines?) But there is also a sense in which it is very different. If it were up to Obama— and it is—this war would be fought entirely by remote control and conducted as if it were a video game.

The drones themselves—the MQ-1 Predator and the MQ-9 Reaper being the weapons of choice—are propeller-driven unmanned aircraft that fly relatively slowly (the Predator cruises at about 80 mph, the Reaper at about 230 mph) and are capable of long endurance. The Predator can fly for 24 hours without refueling, and the Reaper—heavier and faster—for about 14 hours. The Predator carries two 100-pound "Hellfire" missiles, precision-guided munitions with small warheads. The Reaper can carry a combination of Hellfires and larger, 500-pound smart bombs that are sufficient to destroy a house.

Behind them are pilots based in the U.S. and several foreign locations, who rely on satellite reconnaissance and intelligence information from those on the ground.

Drone operators—like most military people—work long hours under considerable stress. But they are non-combatants. Their lives are not at risk, and they don't spend nights hunting terrorists in dark places. They don't, like the Marines, patrol trails and village paths in Afghanistan, braving Taliban fire and IEDs. But as befits Obama's video game war, drone pilots are now eligible for a combat-related medal.

The military awards many medals for bravery in combat, and many more for meritorious non-combat service. But the new Distinguished Warfare medal, to be awarded to drone operators and cyberwar experts, seems to be neither one nor the other. As the Defense Department describes it, a recipient could be a drone operator at Creech Air Force Base, Nevada, flying a drone over Afghanistan, or a soldier at Fort Meade, Maryland, thwarting a cyber attack on a defense network. Yet the Distinguished Warfare medal has been placed higher than both the Purple Heart and the Bronze Star with a for valor in combat.

This rankles the warriors, as well it should. Marine Captain Harold Babbin—my father—finished World War.

II with a Bronze Star with the Combat "V" and a Purple Heart after having fought on Guadalcanal, Tarawa, and Iwo Jima. A non-combat medal outranking the Bronze Star could seem just only to liberals who have no regard for real warriors. In fact, in many ways the drone campaign is liberals' dream war: no combat troops at risk on the ground, at sea, or in the air; no casualties. It's also neat, surgical, and conducted personally by Obama. Such direct presidential involvement in a military campaign is bizarre. In the case of Obama, it's also uncharacteristic. (For the most part, he has distanced himself from the day-to-day conduct of his administration's foreign policy: His new secretary of defense is fumbling through a budget crisis with no guidance from the White House.) Yet an article in the May 26, 2012, New York Times reported that "When a rare opportunity for a drone strike at a top terrorist arises ... it is the president who has reserved to himself the final moral calculation." Wars aren't fought one enemy at a time. Such moral "calculations" only make sense at the presidential level when the question is one of grand strategy, as was the case when Harry Truman decided to use atomic weapons against Japan.

Unfortunately, the debate on the constitutionality and legality of our drone strikes has been more political than substantive. The president has claimed the power to kill any "operational leader" of al Qaeda, even if that person is an American citizen. He has exercised said power on several targets, the two best known being Anwar al-Awlaki, the notorious al Qaeda preacher, and Samir Khan, editor of the al Qaeda magazine Inspire. Both were U.S. citizens. Awlaki was the planner of the attempted "underwear bombing" of a U.S. airliner, and reportedly was involved in Nidal Hasan's Fort Hood mass murder in 2009. Both were killed in a Predator strike in Yemen in September 2011.

Critics on the right and the left are concerned about the constitutionality of killing Americans without the due process guaranteed by the Fifth Amendment. On March 6, Senator Rand Paul filibustered the CIA nomination of John Brennan after the Obama administration refused to say that it could not use a drone to kill an American citizen on U.S. soil.

Paul catapulted himself into the center of the national security debate. That, of course, was too much for Senator John McCain, who begrudgingly agreed that the point was important, but said it shouldn't be made by the "wacko birds" of the Republican Party. The problem is not with Paul but with McCain, who has been virtually the sole Republican spokesman on defense since President Bush left office, and who has been wrong more than he has been right. For example, despite the fact that our law has prohibited the government from torturing anyone since the 1950s, McCain grandstanded a new "anti-torture" law through Congress in 2005 as if it were something new. He succeeded only in making headlines and in making a clear law vague. McCain is more interested in personal promotion than serious discussion, and he needs to be pushed aside.

The constitutional point, though not obvious, is quite large, as Attorney General Holder finally conceded. Under the Fifth Amendment, no person's life can be taken "without due process of law." Further, Executive Order 12333, signed by Ronald Reagan in 1981, bars American intelligence agencies from performing or even participating in assassinations.

A Department of Justice white paper, leaked in January, sets out the administration's legal argument for the drone program. It relies on the 2001 AUMF and several court opinions, and concludes that killing anyone overseas—even American citizens is both legal and constitutional if several criteria are satisfied. First, the target must be a "senior operational leader of al Qaeda or an associated force." Second, an informed "high-level" official of the government must determine that the target poses an imminent, violent threat to the United States. (Later it argues that, because al Qaeda is constantly planning attacks, every al Qaeda operational leader can be presumed to be an imminent threat.) Third, capturing the individual must be infeasible; and fourth, the operation must be conducted consistent with the law of war. The white paper also contends that the lawful killing of an al Qaeda leader is not an assassination. Executive Order 12333 doesn't define "assassination," but the generally accepted definition limits it to politically motivated killings during peacetime. Congress' blanket authorization of force in 2001 allows the administration to overcome this objection.

Before Awlaki was killed, his father sued to bar the government from attacking him. In a 2010 opinion, U.S. District Court Judge John Bates dismissed the case on procedural grounds. But he left the most important questions undecided. First, he alluded that the case might present a political issue beyond the court's jurisdiction. Second, he expressly left open the question of whether the government can "order the assassination of a U.S. citizen without first affording him any form of judicial process whatsoever, based on the mere assertion that he is a dangerous member of a terrorist organization."

Two Supreme Court decisions seem to make the question hazier. In July 1942, eight German saboteurs landed on Long Island and Florida in German uniform, changed quickly into civilian clothes, and were soon captured by the FBI. One was an American citizen who had sworn allegiance to Germany. Later that year, a presidential proclamation declared that any citizens or subjects of a hostile government who entered the U.S. as spies or saboteurs would be tried under military law, not in the civilian courts.

The eight were tried by a military tribunal, and six were sentenced to death. Reviewing the case, the Supreme Court held that none of them, including the purported American (who, having sworn allegiance to Germany, could have been held to have renounced his citizenship), had a habeas corpus right to be tried in a civilian court. They were, in the Court's ruling, properly held as "enemy combatants" subject to military jurisdiction. Sixty-two years later, in Hamdi v. Rumsfeld, the Court ruled that Americans held as "enemy combatants" do in fact have the right to habeas corpus, but it said that a military tribunal would suffice.

In neither case did the Court hold that no due process was guaranteed under the Constitution. Military commissions, for all the criticism of them, clearly provide notice, opportunity to be heard in defense, and all the other indicia of due process. Some have proposed a new court to provide due process to those on Obama's kill list, akin to the Foreign Intelligence Surveillance Act court, which secretly oversees wiretaps and other interceptions of communications under FISA. But to provide adequate due process in the case of a drone strike, such a court would need to give the target advance notice of the attack and an opportunity to oppose the application, which of course would enable the person to escape. So the question remains: Can the U.S. government kill an American citizen without due process?

The answer must be "yes," unless the Constitution is really a suicide note. As Supreme Court rulings, including Hawk, teach us, if the enemy combatant can be captured, he is entitled to due process, including habeas corpus. If he is within the United States, he cannot be killed except by due process of law, including the act of arrest. But as long as he remains a "free range" enemy combatant abroad, the question of whether he can be captured is not for the courts to decide. Such a military operation may be too dangerous for our soliders, too uncertain, or too likely to inflict unacceptable levels of civilian casualties. But those are questions that fall under executive power, not the courts' supervision. We are forced to conclude that Obama's drone program is both legal and constitutional. But is it the right policy?

To draw a conclusion, we must answer two questions: Is it necessary? And is it being conducted the right way? The answer to the first question is dear. Yes, we must take lethal measures against al Qaeda and its "associated forces" everywhere we can find them. Al Qaeda, for all of Obama's protestations to the contrary, is still growing stronger and remains very dangerous to Americans and U.S. interests abroad. In fact, the drone campaign probably is not far-reaching enough.

Our military intelligence and counterterrorism resources are both limited. Not every terrorist group is capable of attacking us, but many are and have done so in the past. It was Hezbollah—the Iranian and Syrian backed group based in Lebanon—that killed 241 Americans in the Beirut barracks bombing of 1983. More recently, Hezbollah fighters attacked Americans in Iraq. And they are probably on the ground in Libya and Afghanistan, too. Iran's Revolutionary Guard Corps killed Americans in Iraq, and they remain one of the most dangerous terrorist forces. Unless and until we contain Iran's nuclear arms program, Obama's global drone war is a necessary part of our counterterrorism efforts.

The second question—whether drone operations are being conducted appropriately—is larger and more important. Strikes on high-level al Qaeda leaders, aimed at decapitating the organization, can reduce our vulnerability to attack, but they can't and won't defeat the enemy. That is the primary defect in Obama's policy.

We cannot defeat Islamist extremism by killing scattered terrorist leaders. If we are to win, we must first identify the enemy and fight in a manner calculated to defeat the ideology that drives him. We are not, and should not be, at war with every believer in Islam. But there is no possibility to peacefully coexist with Islamist terrorists and those nations that harbor them.

The answer is to meet Islamists in ideological battle. Our object should not be to win hearts and minds, but to remind the world of the bankruptcy of an ideology that refuses basic human freedoms. George Bush shied away from the ideological war, which has resulted in more than a decade lost, and Obama has preemptively surrendered.

Three years ago, Obama banned the terms "Islamic extremism" and "jihad" from the official statement of our national security strategy. If we can't use these terms to describe the enemy—even the ones he uses to describe himself—how can we know his mind and defeat his beliefs? In short, under the policies of the Obama administration, we can't.

1. Are there any instances in which the US government has the right to kill an American citizen without due process? Does your answer change if this occurs on American soil?

2. Do you agree that the primary defect in Obama's drone policy is that it will not defeat the enemy?

"HOW OUR OVERLY RESTRICTIVE RULES OF ENGAGEMENT KEEP US FROM WINNING WARS," BY DAVID FRENCH, FROM THE *NATIONAL REVIEW*, DECEMBER 21, 2015

The car was moving at high speed. It had just broken a blockade of American and Iraqi forces and was trying to escape into the gathering dusk. American soldiers, driving larger and slower armored vehicles, mostly the large and unwieldy MRAPs (mine-resistant, ambush-protected vehicles), gave chase. They were intensely interested in the target. Acting on intelligence that high-value al-Qaeda leaders might be present, a cavalry troop — working with Iraqi allies — surrounded an isolated village near the Iranian border. The mission was simple: to search the village and kill or capture identified members of al-Qaeda. It was the kind of mission that the troopers had executed countless times before. It wasn't uncommon to encounter "squirters" — small groups of insurgents who try to sneak or race through American lines and disappear into the desert. Sometimes they were on motorcycles, sometimes on foot, but often they were in cars, armed to the teeth and ready to fight to the death. On occasion the squirters weren't insurgents at all — just harmless, terrified civilians trying to escape a deadly war. This evening, however, our troopers believed that the car ahead wasn't full of civilians. The driver was too skilled, his tactics too knowing for a carload of shepherds. As the car disappeared into the night, the senior officer on the scene radioed for permission to fire. His request went to the TOC, the tactical operations center, which is the beating heart of command and control in the battlefield environment. There the "battle captain," or the senior officer in the chain of command, would decide — shoot or don't shoot.

But first there was a call for the battle captain to make, all the way to brigade headquarters, where a JAG officer — an Army lawyer — was on call 24 hours a day, seven days a week. His job was to analyze the request, apply the governing rules of engagement, and make a recommendation to the chain of command. While the commander made the ultimate decision, he rarely contradicted JAG recommendations. After all, if soldiers opened fire after a lawyer had deemed the attack outside the rules, they would risk discipline — even prosecution — if the engagement went awry. Acting on the best available information — including a description of the suspect vehicle, a description of its tactics, analysis of relevant intelligence, and any available video feeds — the JAG officer had to determine whether there was sufficient evidence of "hostile intent" to authorize the use of deadly force. He had to make a life-or-death decision in mere minutes. In this case, the lawyer said no — insufficient evidence. No deadly force. Move to detain rather than shoot to kill. The commander deferred. No shot. Move to detain. So the chase continued, across roads and open desert. The suspect vehicle did its best to shake free, but at last it was cornered by converging American forces. There was no escape. Four men emerged from the car. American soldiers dismounted from their MRAPs, and with one man in the lead, weapons raised, they ordered the Iraqis to surrender. Those who were in the TOC that night initially thought someone had stepped on a land mine. Watching on video feed, they saw the screen go white, then black. For several agonizing minutes, no one knew what had happened. Then the call came. Suicide bomber. One of the suspects had self-detonated, and Americans were hurt. One badly — very badly. Despite desperate efforts to save his life, he died just before he arrived at a functioning aid station. Another casualty of the rules of engagement.

Imagine if the United States had fought World War II with a mandate to avoid any attack when civilians were likely to be present. Imagine Patton's charge through Western Europe constrained by granting the SS safe haven whenever it sheltered among civilians. If you can imagine this reality, then you can also imagine a world without a D-Day, a world where America's greatest generals are war criminals, and where the mighty machinery of Hitler's industrial base produces planes, tanks, and guns unmolested. In other words, you can imagine a world where our Army is a glorified police force and our commanders face prosecution for fighting a real war. That describes our wars in Iraq and Afghanistan. For more than a decade, complaints about the rules of engagement have bubbled up on soldiers' message boards, in stray comments — often by soldiers' parents — on conservative websites, and in the occasional article in the mainstream press. Frequently, this comes in the context of lauding the military for its restraint. Yet despite being such a vital — and sometimes decisive — factor in a more than decade-long war, the rules of engagement are still poorly understood, and their impact is largely unknown. As ISIS continues to grow and its reach expands from the Middle East to Europe, the United States, and beyond, it's time to consider the true cost of America's self-imposed constraints.

Rules of engagement are separate from — but related to — the actual law of armed conflict. The law of armed conflict (LOAC) is a comprehensive, complex body of law developed largely by the Western powers in an effort to render war more humane. Its principles are relatively simple — designed to limit the use of force to military targets and to treat captives with proper care and respect — but have become almost mind-numbingly complex in application. The Department of Defense's new Law of War Manual stretches to a staggering 1,176 pages and purports not just to define general principles but also to govern specific applications in a granular level of detail. But no soldier, no commander, and indeed few military lawyers can master these rules in all their complexity. And so they learn generalities. In general, the LOAC is now governed by the principles of necessity, humanity, proportionality, and distinction. The principle of necessity, to quote the Law of War Manual, "justifies certain actions necessary to defeat the enemy as quickly and efficiently as possible." Humanity "forbids actions unnecessary to achieve that object." Proportionality requires that even when actions may be justified by military necessity, such actions must not be unreasonable or excessive. Distinction imposes on the parties an obligation to distinguish between military and civilian targets and to facilitate distinctions by clearly marking military personnel and military vehicles.

In his introductory letter to the Law of War Manual, Department of Defense general counsel Stephen Preston declares the law of war to be "part of our military heritage" and says that "obeying it is the right thing to do." He further argues that the doctrines are no impediment to "fighting well and prevailing." In other words, these legal doctrines are said to allow American soldiers to fight under the highest of moral standards and still win wars.

These are noble principles, but unfortunately their applicability peaked more than a century ago, when warring states in Europe — exhausted by the Wars of Religion — fought battles on open fields between militaries wearing the most distinctive of uniforms. Think of the battle of Waterloo in what is now Belgium or, here in the United States, the battles of Gettysburg and Chancellorsville. The United States hasn't fought a conflict governed by the law of war in almost a century. Indeed, just as the law of war is part of America's military heritage, so is the modern concept of "total war" — a nation mobilizes its full resources to destroy not just the military of an opposing country but also its very capacity to wage war. America's enemies, more-over, have consistently and flagrantly disregarded the laws of war. Arguably, the United States has not fought a nation that substantially complied with the LOAC since it squared off against the Germans in the trenches of Western Europe in World War I. Instead, both the regular armies (Nazis, Japanese, North Koreans, Chinese, and North Vietnamese) and the insurgencies (Viet Cong, Taliban, and al-Qaeda) have brazenly violated the law at every turn.

The modern result is a military farce. American forces play by the rules while our enemies exploit those same rules to limit our freedom of action, create sanc-tuaries where they can rest and rearm, and then launch international propaganda campaigns when our pains-taking targeting proves to be the least bit imprecise. Yet — and here's the crucial point — through their rules of engagement, American soldiers don't just comply with the law of war. They go beyond the requirements of the LOAC to impose additional and legally unnecessary restrictions on the use of military force. Rules of engagement represent true war-by-wonk, in which a deadly brew of lawyers, politicians, soldiers, and social scientists endeavors to fine-tune the use of military force to somehow kill the enemy while "winning over" the local population even as the local population is in the direct line of fire.

Defenders of the rules of engagement often speak as if they represent nothing more than military common sense — after all, wouldn't it be better if American soldiers killed only insurgents? Don't civilian deaths inflame the population? General Stanley McChrystal famously told his troops in Afghanistan that they should spend 95 percent of their time "building relationships" and "meeting the needs" of the Afghan people. Only 5 percent should be spent fighting the Taliban.

In establishing these priorities, McChrystal was purporting to apply the counterinsurgency principle of "protecting the population," but it is difficult to protect a population when the rules of engagement grant the enemy enormous freedom of movement and access to civilians and civilian sites. By imposing restrictive rules of engagement, McChrystal (like commanders before and since) was making it more difficult for his troops both to clear the Taliban from towns and villages and to hold territory against inevitable counterattacks. Counterinsurgency is always long and painful, but when troops are unable to clear and hold territory, they can't truly enter the important "build" phase, in which soldiers transition from constant combat to supporting local allies and building local militaries in an environment relatively free of threat. Thus, rather than learning and applying the true laws of war, soldiers are taught an absurd distortion of them — rules that have grown more restrictive throughout the War on Terror, culminating most recently in the Obama administration's reported decisions in the air war against ISIS to leave known military targets intact for fear of inflicting even a single civilian death.

While the precise rules of engagement in any given theater of operations tend to be classified, their general parameters are well known and give American soldiers the option of using force only in the face of a "hostile act" or "hostile intent," or when an enemy fighter has been "positively identified." Once the enemy is engaged, the rules then govern the types of weapons that may be used, how they may be used, where they may be used, and the various levels of command that can authorize the use of each kind of weapon. So unless a soldier is using his personal weapons system to engage an enemy who is actively firing on him, there is all too often confusion and delay on the battlefield. Sometimes troops must consult lawyers even during active firefights. The results are often grim. Americans die.

I revealed the time and location for the meeting of an al-Qaeda leader with an operational cell specializing in improvised explosive devices (IEDs). The location was a village in Diyala province, north of the town of Balad Ruz. The time was just after noon on Friday. But there was a problem — a big problem: The meeting was in a mosque, and the al-Qaeda leader was the imam. While tribal leaders pleaded for American forces to strike, Army lawyers were writing legal memos, sending requests for permission to raid the mosque (complete with legal arguments) up the chain of command. The clock ticked as the command deliberated. Finally, the word came: Permission denied. The potential secondary effects of a raid — complete with possible visuals of American soldiers storming a mosque — outweighed the benefits of an attack. But there are also effects of not acting. Days later, an American patrol was attacked by a massive, remote-detonated IED. A Humvee reinforced with extra armor was blown into the air. Four Americans died. One soldier miraculously escaped, but with crippling, life-altering injuries. The IED cell had struck again. The effects continued. Within weeks of the IED strike, the cell ambushed another American patrol — this time with elements of the al-Qaeda group firing from, yes, a mosque. One American was seriously injured, and the resulting firefight lasted 36 hours, inflicting massive damage. Much of the village was destroyed as American and al-Qaeda troops traded fire, locked in house-to-house combat. The rules of engagement saved a mosque but destroyed a village — and likely four more American lives.

Talk to combat veterans and the stories like this will come pouring out, often variations on the same theme: We knew where the enemy was, but we couldn't pursue him. And when we fought him, we couldn't kill him. Bing West, a retired Marine infantry officer, the author of multiple books on the War on Terror, and a journalist who has embedded over two dozen times with troops on the ground in Iraq and Afghanistan, believes the rules of engagement often rob American soldiers of their military advantage. With body armor, ammunition, and other gear weighing in excess of 90 pounds, infantry can't "press home attacks," West says. "Fire and maneuver does not exist, so troops have to apply massive firepower." Yet the rules block access to the firepower needed to win engagements.

Few engagements show this reality more starkly than the battle of Ganjgal, featured in the book West co-authored with Medal of Honor recipient Dakota Meyer, Into the Fire. Members of Meyer's small team of Marine advisers to an Afghan-army unit walked into a Taliban ambush and soon found themselves pinned down, unable to effectively return fire or safely retreat. In prior wars — indeed, earlier in the Afghan War — this was exactly the time when Marines could call for artillery support or an air strike and use the American military's immense firepower advantage not only to save their own lives but to destroy the attacking enemy force. But not this time. Under the rules of engagement, the directive was clear: "Do not employ 'air-to-ground or indirect fires against residential compounds, defined as any structure or building known or likely to contain civilians, unless the ground force commander has verified that no civilians are present.'" Marines watched F-15E Eagles circle, impotently. Artillery was silent. In the meantime, Meyer launched a desperate effort — with Army captain Will Swenson — to find and rescue his lost comrades. Meyer rescued Afghan allies and fought — sometimes hand to hand — to reach his team, only to find it was too late. His friends, his brothers, were dead.

As West notes, "you cannot fight a major battle with the current rules of engagement." Some units were so paralyzed in their ability to mount offensive operations that they were reduced to rolling outside of their base and waiting to be fired upon. Only then was it truly clear that they could respond, though not with the full power at their disposal, and so long as civilians were likely present, they were often prohibited from responding even with the precision-guided weapons that make the American military theoretically the deadliest in the world.

In Iraq and Syria, American pilots have watched as ISIS fighters moved freely among civilians, and they've held fire rather than bomb ISIS oil trucks that are funding the jihadist war, out of concern that some of the truck drivers might not be jihadists. In one notorious incident, pilots dropped leaflets to warn of an imminent attack and made fake bombing runs to try to clear the area of civilians. Indeed, the fake bombing run is common enough that insurgents now understand that "fly-bys" can be a signal not of imminent doom but rather of safety. After all, if they were in real danger, the bomb would have already dropped. By some reports, up to 75 percent of sorties end without dropping bombs, and West reports that some pilots fear court-martial if they don't adequately question a ground controller's request for a strike. Here's the final irony of our concern for the laws of war and civilian casualties: Our rules of engagement not only create an additional incentive for enemy law-breaking, they ultimately lead to mass-scale civilian casualties at the hands of unconstrained jihadists.

Fully aware of American restrictions, enemy fighters not only refuse to wear uniforms, they often do their best to blend in with the civilian population, eschewing distinctive dress, armbands, or any other insignia that brands them as members of a terrorist militia. Rather than congregate in isolated outposts, they cluster in mosques, around hospitals, and even in private homes. While such tactics are frequent in guerrilla warfare, they are neither legal nor moral, and our jihadist opponents have reached appalling lows even by the rough and brutal standards of insurgencies. During my deployment in Iraq, I watched on live feed as a fleeing insurgent picked up a small child and carried him as a human shield to escape pursuing forces. I've seen al-Qaeda cells hold meetings in the courtyards of farmhouses while surrounded by young children. And so they live to fight — and kill — again. Civilians in jihadist-held areas are shot, stabbed, crucified, burned alive, beheaded, and thrown from tall buildings. When they take new cities, jihadists fire indiscriminately in civilian areas, often killing anything that moves. To keep their oppressive peace, they sometimes massacre entire villages. As a result, in its own military campaigns, America often saves the few only to watch the many die horrific deaths.

American military success has been tied to looser rules of engagement. From the initial lightning march through Iraq to Baghdad, to the decisive battles of the Iraq troop surge, American forces win when they take the gloves off. Though most "routine" operations during the Surge were covered by the now-standard rules of engagement, resulting in the tragic incidents described above, during key battles, commanders often loosened the rules, granting greater discretion to leaders in the field and more freedom of action to soldiers to identify and engage the enemy. For example, soldiers were empowered to engage the enemy whenever they encountered known enemy tactics, techniques, and procedures (known as "TTPs"), even when no weapons were evident. And the number and nature of identified TTPs was expanded to encompass the latest intelligence.

Indeed, as the Surge indicates, the choice isn't between the mass destruction of total war and the purported surgical precision and humanity of wonk war. Seasoned American veterans can and do make good decisions under pressure. They can distinguish friend from foe in a complex battlefield. They wield their weapons with precision and skill. Intentional killing of civilians is exceedingly rare. Of course war is never easy, and choices are always fraught with danger. Loosening the rules of engagement and delegating greater authority to the troops in the field will likely lead to increased civilian casualties, but granting warriors the ability to close with, and destroy, opposing forces has proven to diminish enemy combat power, clear civilian areas of enemy influence, and enable soldiers to hold on to hard-fought gains. While JAG officers' concern with the terrible consequences of poor decision-making under pressure is well meaning and understandable, the current rules have effectively taken combat decision-making away from experienced warriors and put it in the hands of far less experienced lawyers. Again and again, lawyers prevent warriors from engaging targets the warriors know are hostile but cannot prove to the standards required by the relevant rules. Moreover, no true oversight exists. Political leaders increasingly don't understand the military, much less the weapons and tactics needed to prevail on the battlefield. Every branch of government blanches in the face of left-wing critics who speak as if by reflex of "war crimes" any time civilians die.

To be sure, reforming the rules of engagement will not by itself lead to American victory in the War on Terror, particularly because it confronts an amorphous group of violent religious ideologues rather than a fixed set of powers. But reforming the rules of engagement will make the American military more effective wherever and however that happens. The Left is fond of claiming that the outcome of American military engagements in Iraq and Afghanistan reveals the "profound limitations" of American military power. In reality, however, they reveal only the profound limitations of a military so lawyered up that it can't drop a bomb or fire an artillery round without a J.D. on the line. Our enemies—who disregard every limit in their quest to kill, destroy, and expand the scope of their striking power — benefit, and are delighted. ISIS is seeking to deploy chemical weapons. America is looking for excuses not to drop bombs. In this circumstance, soldiers and families suffer. Mothers lose their children. Wives lose their husbands. Soldiers lose their brothers. The holes in our hearts are gaping, and the psychic wounds are made rawer by the fact that so many of those losses were unnecessary. I knew men who died because lawyers and politicians failed them. Those who served, and their loved ones, are left to pick up the pieces, visiting graves, comforting families, and feeling a deep and lasting sorrow. Our nation doesn't trust its warriors, and its warriors are paying the price.

1. "Legal warfare" may sound like a contradiction in terms. Yet, the author claims that US forces are in fact hindered by their accountability to lawyers. Does this strike you as a widespread problem?

2. The author also argues that our enemies do not recognize the distinction between civilians and combatants. Therefore, while US forces should not deliberately harm civilians, neither should they worry excessively about them. Yet, isn't this precisely the definition of "terror" we wish to defeat? In other words, what's more important, winning by any means necessary, or adhering to basic human standards of decency?

CHAPTER 4

WHAT ADVOCATES SAY

This chapter examines a few viewpoints on US engagement in the Middle East held by advocates from various points of the political spectrum. Three main positions emerge as we survey this landscape: neoconservative, so-called "realist," and leftist.

On the right, commentator Tim Kane tries to recuperate unilateral US action, primarily military occupation. Regardless of possible efficacy, this idea has fallen wildly out of favor with the general public, particularly after more than a decade of military debacles in Iraq and Afghanistan. Therefore, it is unlikely that this hawkish position will gain traction, unless an existential threat to the US surfaces.

Another familiar and tenacious neoconservative argument is the unconditional defense of the state of Israel. John Podhoretz argues this line with a passionate condemnation of former president Obama's nuclear deal with Iran, which he believes is tantamount to an abandonment of Israel. Whether his admonishment convinces will depend on one's feelings about Israel's policies and long-term security.

Advocates on the left are less brazen. Writing on behalf of the liberal Center for American Progress, expert Brian Katulis delineates a comprehensive plan to contain ISIS and restore stability to the region that we might call "realist." Though these recommendations are quite detailed, it is debatable whether the specifics of their plan are concrete enough to put into action. Finally, Stanley Heller sketches what a leftist, humanitarian, internationalist perspective on the Syrian conflict might look like. Eschewing easy answers, Heller reminds us that the lesser of two evils is still evil. Heller steers clear of geopolitical answers, choosing instead to focus on how US citizens can withdraw support for oppressive regimes.

"THE EMERGENCY," BY JOHN PODHORETZ, FROM *COMMENTARY*, APRIL 1, 2015

We have entered a state of emergency. The Obama administration is pursuing policies that effectively serve the purposes of one of America's greatest foes and treat one of America's dearest friends as though it were an adversary.

The White House has implicitly taken up the cause of normalizing Iran and has become at the very least complicit in the international goal of isolating Israel.

Barack Obama has decided the key to his legacy is a deal with the Islamic Republic of Iran that will enshrine its nuclear capacity but delay its ability to build and deploy a bomb for a time—that is, assuming Iran doesn't cheat, which is an assumption that requires a leap of geopolitical faith Blaise Pascal would have blanched at. Meanwhile, 970 miles from Tehran, the State of Israel finds itself the unwanted focus of another Obama legacy effort: the effort to drive a wedge between the two countries and thereby realign America's interests in the Middle East away from Israel's interests.

In making clear his desire to establish a working relationship with a nation that does not abide by any standards of civilized conduct, a nation that oppresses in medieval fashion at home and that is the worst state sponsor of terrorism abroad, the president is tacitly accepting the everyday behavior and casting a blind eye on the plain language of one of the world's most monstrous regimes.

"There is a practical streak to the Iranian regime," the president told Thomas L. Friedman of the *New York Times* on April 5. "There [is] an appetite among the Iranian people for a rejoining with the international community, an emphasis on the economics and the desire to link up with a global economy. And so what we've seen over the last several years, I think, is the opportunity for those forces within Iran that want to break out of the rigid framework that they have been in for a long time to move in a different direction. It's not a radical break, but it's one that I think offers us the chance for a different type of relationship."

The overall purpose here is to remake the geopolitical map and include Iran among the nations with which we can and should do business. From this perspective, Iran's systematic record of anti-Americanism and anti-Semitism and its role as the world's most active state sponsor of terrorism are not bugs but features: Iran is important not only because it is an oil-rich state with religious and ideological ambitions, but also because it has set itself against the United States and the West. And so it must be attended to, its concerns taken seriously, its desires and wishes accorded respect. In Obama's view, it is with adversaries that America must enmesh itself to find some form of common ground.

This theory has governed most of the Obama administration's foreign-policy approaches over the past six years, from the Russian reset to the opening to Cuba. The corollary is that little or no positive attention needs to be paid to allies, especially if those allies are inconveniently situated either geographically or ideologically. Thus, in 2009, Obama had no problem abrogating the long-standing deal to put missile-defense systems in Poland and the Czech Republic, even though they are two stalwart friends of the United States, because they interfered with his efforts to improve the American relationship with Vladimir Putin.

Even those countries that we should not call our friends but with which many of our national interests align are to be consigned to the second ring of concern. Thus, while the president speaks gently of Iran and draws parallels between its politics and ours—it is a "complicated country," he said to Friedman, "just as America is a complicated country"—he offers systematic criticism of the internal dynamics of the Sunni Arab nations in the Middle East that have expressed alarm over the thaw: "I think the biggest threats that they face may not be coming from Iran invading. It's going to be from dissatisfaction inside their own countries."

The Obama policy of behaving high-handedly toward friends and charitably toward foes is most striking in the case of the State of Israel. The president and his people speak with barely disguised disgust about the policies of a friendly government and rough election-day tactics in a vibrant democracy in which 72.3 percent of those eligible to vote did so. They talk of re visiting the relationship with Israel, reevaluating it—all of which is code-speak for withdrawing American protection from Israel in the international bodies that wish to do it injury. It was not mere chance that these two legacy policies converged in the month of March 2015. Something more sinister was at work.

The results of Israel's election on March 17 were disappointing to the president and his team, given how tirelessly they had worked to undermine the eventually victorious Netanyahu. A key Obama campaign aide named Jeremy Bird had been dispatched to the Holy Land to manage a get-out-the-vote group called V15 whose sole campaign message was "Anyone But Bibi." In the end, Netanyahu's Likud party garnered 30 seats, as opposed to the 18 seats it had won just two years earlier—a result that has to be seen as a conscious rebuke of Obama's effort to unseat the Israeli prime minister. In choosing not to reject Netanyahu but to strengthen him, Israelis effectively endorsed the views of Obama's most dangerous critic—the only democratically elected leader on earth who might find it necessary to act drastically to save his country in a way that would scuttle Obama's vision for the future of the Middle East.

Netanyahu has made it clear that he cannot stand by while a course is charted to a future in which Iran can build and deploy a nuclear weapon, given that its millenarian leaders have vowed to wipe Israel off the map. But under the terms of the strange April 2 agreement-with-Iran-that-is-not-really-an-agreement—terms we know the president had already conceded well before the Israeli elections on March 17—Obama has effectively endorsed a future in which Iran will have the power and the means to do exactly that.

Shockingly, on April 5, Obama acknowledged to NPR that at best the deal keeps Iran from going nuclear for a dozen years. (He did so unprompted by the interviewer, suggesting that for a moment the president had come under the spell cast on Jim Carrey in *Liar Liar* to speak the truth even when it would harm him to do so.) Forget about cheating: Even that 12-year delay will come about only if Iran hews to every particular of the terms Obama and Secretary of State John Kerry announced so triumphantly on April 2. Obama surely knows Iran is unlikely to assent to those terms in the final agreement to be signed on June 30—because a) Iran instantly began balking at the specifics we laid out and b) if those terms had been acceptable, the deal could have been signed and sealed in Switzerland. And yet Obama also felt free to tell Friedman that "this is our best bet by far to make sure Iran doesn't get a nuclear weapon." The man who said "if you like your doctor, you can keep your doctor" when he knew it was untrue is repurposing the ObamaCare communications strategy for the Iran deal.

It is unquestionable that the understanding Obama's underlings reached with Iran will at the very least permit the Islamic Republic to retain a stockpile of uranium, the advanced devices that can convert it into the guts of a bomb in a matter of months, and the facilities in which to do it. We are told Iran has agreed to dilute the uranium, put the centrifuges in a locked closet, and call its hardened bunker at Fordow "a research center."

For the hard work of accepting such a deal, Iran will receive tens of billions of dollars in payoff money it can use for other purposes, thus freeing up resources to continue its work on military applications of nuclear technology if that suits the mullahs.

But look, Obama says. The deal-that's-not-a-deal means Iran won't be nuclear for a while yet, and the Iranians probably don't mean it when they say they will destroy Israel, and even if they do, so what, because they'll never try it, and you know what, if they do try it, America will "have Israel's back." Which sounds nice, but is useless as a basis for policy, since in the aftermath of a nuclear strike, Israel will not have a back for America to have, only tens if not hundreds of thousands dead and/or sickened unto death.

And this is the point. Of all the things on earth Obama does not have, "Israel's back" ranks close to the top. For somehow, over the course of the nine years the world has been grappling with the Iranian nuclear threat, the goals of the United States have been defined downward—from prevention to containment. We have gone from insisting we had to keep Iran from becoming a nuclear power (something the president declared unconditionally he would not allow to happen) to adopting a policy designed to manage Iran's existence as one.

The term of art is that Iran has now become, and will remain, a "threshold nuclear power." Some threshold: According to the president, Iran can cross it in two months. Obama says the deal—if there is a deal and if that deal is adhered to—will lengthen the distance across the threshold to a year, for another dozen years. In year 13, the threshold disappears. But 2028 is a long time from now. We'll all be driving flying cars and living on Venus by then.

There are several reasons the original goal of preventing Iran from acquiring a nuclear weapon altogether was absolutely necessary—among them, to forestall a Sunni-Shia nuclear-arms race in the Middle East and to keep a revolutionary terror-supporting anti-American regime from becoming a first-order world power. Practically, however, the threat an Iranian nuke poses was and is primarily to one country—a country Iran's former president continually said would soon cease to exist. Now, lest one think the goal of Israel's destruction retired along with Mahmoud Ahmadinejad in 2013, please note that the leader of its religious police militia said on March 30 that the aim of "erasing Israel off the map" is "nonnegotiable." So the danger an Iranian nuke poses to the good working order of the world is profound. It will reorder military and strategic priorities in a profoundly destabilizing way over the course of this century. But the danger a deployed Iranian nuke poses to millions of Israelis is instantaneous. And we should not balk at speaking the truth: Should a pact with Iran be signed, Barack Obama will be complicit in the act of casting a nuclear shadow over the future of the Jewish people, whose continued existence on this earth could not survive a mushroom cloud over Tel Aviv—which would constitute a second Holocaust within living memory of the first.

This terrifying truth is at the core of the warning Benjamin Netanyahu has been delivering about the Iranian threat for six years now—the warning against the temptation to believe it will be acceptable for Iran to go nuclear. Obama has surrendered to that temptation. He has now made an Iranian bomb acceptable. Was the accuracy of Netanyahu's characterization the true cause of Obama's astonishingly vituperative response to Netanyahu's conduct in the days leading up to the Israeli election? First Netanyahu acknowledged to an interviewer that current Palestinian conduct meant there would be no Palestinian state during his premiership—which is the truth and nothing but the truth, though it is a truth fantasists are loath to acknowledge and one that those who believe peace will be served by the creation of such a state as soon as possible find galling to hear.

Then, on election day, Netanyahu engaged in a profoundly ill-advised get-out-the-vote tactic by warning in vulgar terms of increased Arab-Israeli participation. That was distasteful and inappropriate, but it was far less ugly than election-day moves during other elections in other democratic countries whose results Obama has welcomed and celebrated in years past.

No matter. Obama's press secretary, Josh Earnest, said Netanyahu's words about Arab voters "turning out in droves" were so horrific they "undermine the values and democratic ideals that have been important to our democracy and an important part of what binds the United States and Israel together." Indeed, those words coupled with what the prime minister had said about Palestinian statehood triggered a phone call in which, according to a White House official speaking to

Reuters, "the president told the prime minister that we will need to reassess our options following the prime minister's new positions and comments regarding the two-state solution."

Even after Netanyahu clarified his remarks and said he believed the best future for Israel was a two-state solution, the White House did not relent. "We do take him at his word," said the press secretary before saying they didn't take him at his word: "But he was quite clear that he did not envision a scenario where a Palestinian state would be established while he was the prime minister of Israel.... And his lack of commitment to what has been the foundation of our policymaking in the region means that the United States should rightfully reevaluate the kinds of policy decisions that we make as it relates to the Middle East. And that's what the president has said he will do."

Let us be clear about what the White House is considering. It is threatening to cease protecting Israel from the jackals at the United Nations and other international organizations. These words from the Obama administration came the same week that the UN's Commission on the Status of Women singled out Israel—alone among the UN's 193 member nations—as the worst abuser of women's rights in the world. In brief, Obama is signaling his desire to Europeanize American policy toward Israel. Two weeks later, Obama told Friedman: "It has been personally difficult for me to hear ... expressions that somehow ... this administration has not done everything it could to look out for Israel's interest." Why? "Because of the deep affinities that I feel for the Israeli people and for the Jewish people." Translation: Some of my best friends are Jewish.

Many liberal American Jews think of Obama as their friend. He is not—not the friend of any Jew who understands his people are under unique and unprecedented threat. Obama is working to strengthen not only Iran's hand but also the hand of those in the United States who believe the relationship between the U.S. and the Jewish state should be cleaved.

Nor is Obama a friend of Israel, for his policies are now aiding and abetting the nation that poses a literally apocalyptic danger to the Jewish people. If this deal is signed on June 30, Barack Obama will have made the world a far less safe and far more dangerous place—and by signing it, he will have signaled his willingness to see the Jewish future sacrificed on the altar of his own ambitions.

The threat is not immediate. The emergency is.

1. Do you take Iran's threat to "wipe Israel off the map" at face value? Does an unprovoked nuclear strike against a sovereign nation (and one supported by the US at that) seem as likely as the author fears?

2. Are there other reasons why this nuclear deal may be a bad idea? Or do you think (as perhaps former president Obama does) that integrating Iran into the global economy will diminish their belligerent tendencies?

"DEFEATING ISIS: AN INTEGRATED STRATEGY TO ADVANCE MIDDLE EAST STABILITY," BY BRIAN KATULIS, HARDIN LANG, AND VIKRAM SINGH, FROM THE *CENTER FOR AMERICAN PROGRESS*, SEPTEMBER 10, 2014

U.S. airstrikes in Iraq against the Islamic State of Iraq and al-Sham, or ISIS, have been an important step to contain the rise of the extremist group, respond to immediate threats to U.S. citizens in Iraq, and prevent possible acts of genocide. These airstrikes enabled Iraqis to resist ISIS and bought time for the Iraqi government to begin building a more inclusive administration under a new prime minister, Haider al-Abadi.* But as the Center for American Progress noted in a June report, U.S. military action needs to be just one part of a long-term multinational political and security strategy in the region.

The new strategy should aim to contain and degrade ISIS and enable regional partners to continue to build the tools needed to defeat ISIS's movement with international support. This report outlines actions to advance three core strategic goals:

1. Contain and degrade the threat ISIS poses to the Middle East region and global security

2. Alleviate the humanitarian crisis affecting millions of Syrians and Iraqis

3. Restore the territorial integrity of Iraq and Syria

The ISIS threat is eroding the borders of both Iraq and Syria, and it represents an immediate and significant threat to the surrounding region. ISIS also represents an evolving threat to the United States, Europe, and global security in the form of international terrorism enabled by the group's thousands of foreign fighters and its abundance of cash and military resources. An environment of chaos and great suffering has allowed ISIS to emerge. The conflict in Syria alone has created the largest humanitarian crisis the world has faced in decades. Some 9 million Syrians have fled their homes, and 3 million Syrians are now refugees, making them the world's largest refugee population and placing a tremendous burden on neighboring countries, such as Jordan, Lebanon, and Turkey.

As with efforts to counter extremism elsewhere, defeating ISIS will require a concentrated effort over time. Any successful U.S. strategy must be built on a foundation of regional cooperation that requires coordinated action from U.S. partners—a central concept of the Counterterrorism Partnership Fund that President Barack Obama proposed earlier this year. The strategy will be multifaceted, involving intelligence cooperation, security support, vigorous regional and international diplomacy, strategic communications and public diplomacy, and political engagement.

While military action alone will be insufficient to defeat ISIS, the United States and other nations may need to undertake airstrikes and provide military assistance to disrupt and degrade ISIS in Syria. These strikes should be conducted in concert with regional and international partners. Ideally, such airstrikes would receive the support from the United Nations or—absent action to authorize the use of force by the U.N. Security Council—from a coalition of America's Gulf partners and North Atlantic Treaty Organization, or NATO, allies. As always, the United States should reserve the right to undertake unilateral military action to defend the homeland or protect U.S. personnel from imminent harm. Whether unilaterally or with partners, U.S. military strikes should be limited in terms of scope and duration and under clear oversight of Congress. As CAP said in June when it advocated for action against ISIS in Iraq, "The United States should not undertake military action lightly and should be wary of unintended consequences. But not all military action is the same. Ground troops or invasions to control a country are very different from limited air strikes or targeted assistance to help push back terrorist extremists."

Focusing too much on direct U.S. military action in the fight against ISIS ignores the equally important diplomatic and economic steps that will be required to defeat this extremist group. U.S. military strikes or even boots on the ground cannot defeat ISIS alone and could become a rallying cry and recruitment tool for extremists, repeating one of the most costly strategic errors of the 2003 Iraq War. At the same time, building a unified, committed coalition to effectively degrade ISIS will require intense diplomatic and military leadership from the United States to mobilize and coordinate partners. The United States must leverage its unique capabilities in the military, security assistance, and intelligence arenas. Working together, nations committed to defeating ISIS should take concerted action to empower regional and local forces to fight back against ISIS terrorism.

A successful U.S. strategy will require reinvigorated support for Syrian opposition forces to establish a third way that is opposed to President Bashar al-Assad's regime on one side and ISIS on the other. This reinvigorated support should include the $500 million of additional assistance that President Obama proposed in June. With 10 nations agreeing to work together against ISIS during the NATO summit in Wales and the Arab League announcing a joint commitment to fight ISIS, the foundation for such international cooperation is taking shape. These countries—including the United Kingdom, Germany, Turkey, Saudi Arabia, and the United Arab Emirates—should match their commitment on paper with financial and material resources to complement the resources committed by the United States in the fight against ISIS.

AN INTEGRATED STRATEGY TO DEGRADE AND DEFEAT ISIS AND ADVANCE STABILITY IN THE MIDDLE EAST

ISIS's advances this summer have made Iraq and Syria part of the same battlefield, erasing the international border and turning the regional struggles for power into a substantial threat to international peace and security. The United States should advance its three core goals noted above by focusing on the following pillars:

- Building and managing an international coalition to defeat ISIS and stabilize the region
- Increasing support for Iraq's political, economic, and security transitions, in particular with a revived U.S.-Iraq Strategic Framework Agreement
- Initiating a more concerted effort to end Syria's civil war and support the creation of a transitional government

PILLAR I: BUILDING AND MANAGING COALITIONS TO DEFEAT ISIS AND STABILIZE THE REGION

The United States should not confront the threat posed by ISIS alone. The international and regional coalition against ISIS should look more like the 1991 Gulf War or the post-9/11 coalition against Al Qaeda and the Taliban and less like the 2003 Iraq War coalition. Secretary of State John Kerry's and U.S. Defense Secretary Chuck Hagel's visits to the region to press for coordinated action are a good start. To follow up, the United States should designate a specific U.S. government lead or a small interagency team to manage the building and sustaining of an anti-ISIS coalition. There is no playbook for this sort of effort, and the United States should operate on three levels: with actors in the region, with transatlantic partners and other core allies, and through the United Nations.

REGIONAL COOPERATION

The United States should propose that states in the region commit to common principles and specific, coordinated actions to help isolate and counter ISIS and better respond to the humanitarian catastrophe. This will not be easy as the Sunni-Shia sectarian divide in the region is now accompanied by growing tensions between leading Sunni-majority states. In addition, key countries in the region lack some basic capacities needed for operational impact, as demonstrated by the failure of regional efforts to support elements of the anti-Assad opposition in Syria. While the United States and other countries may need to fill such capability gaps, regional partners should contribute financial and other resources to support a multinational effort. With partners in the region, the United States can take the following steps:

- **Create an ISIS-focused intelligence fusion cell in the region.** The United States has a wide range of networked relationships with key Middle East intelligence services. Jordan is a close partner in counterterrorism efforts throughout the Middle East and outside the region in places such as Afghanistan. Saudi intelligence services have been battling certain Islamist extremist groups, such as ISIS and al-Nusra Front—the Al Qaeda affiliate now dominating parts of the battlefield. The Turkish National Intelligence Organization also has extensive intelligence contacts and specialized knowledge of the various extremist groups operating in northern Syria. The United States would need to provide the backbone for any regional intelligence fusion effort.
- **Establish a multi-agency and multinational ISIS threat finance cell to target the economic base of ISIS.** ISIS funds its activities from areas under its control through taxation, illicit economies such as oil smuggling and extortion, and external support, mainly from individuals in Gulf states. Some estimates project ISIS will raise between $100 million and $200 million over the next year. To disrupt ISIS's finances, the United States should work with regional partners to target the criminal networks that ISIS uses to sell goods or otherwise generate revenue; disrupt ISIS oil extraction, transport, and refining operations and prevent exchanges with buyers in foreign markets such as Iran, Turkey, and the Kurdistan Regional Government, or KRG; and disrupt online and regional fundraising efforts. The United States should create

an interagency threat finance cell headed by either
the U.S. Treasury Department or State Department
with military and intelligence personnel, and it should
be based in the region to help coordinate the
collection and analysis of financial and
economic intelligence.

- **Coordinate security assistance to national and
  subnational actors fighting ISIS and al-Nusra Front
  on the ground in Syria and Iraq.** The United States
  has already stepped up its direct military assistance
  to Iraqi Kurdish forces and has proposed an additional $500 million to support select members of the
  Syrian opposition. These efforts should be incorpo-
  rated into a regional plan. In many instances, the
  most capable security partners will likely be found at
  the subnational level, including tribes, and U.S partners in the region will have deeper ties and greater
  ability to provide support to such forces fighting ISIS.
  A joint State Department and Defense Department
  team should coordinate these efforts.
- **Airstrikes and surveillance in support of regional
  forces and local ground forces fighting ISIS and
  al-Nusra Front.** In targeted instances, the United
  States—and if possible, a broader coalition of
  allies—should conduct direct military airstrikes
  against ISIS and other radical groups operating in
  Syria and Iraq. These strikes should be conducted as
  part of a regional or international coalition under a
  multilateral framework with congressional
  authorization and oversight.

A TRANSATLANTIC AND ALLIED RESPONSE TO ISIS

The September 2014 NATO summit took several steps to energize the transatlantic community to confront ISIS. Nine countries pledged to join U.S. efforts to counter ISIS, but no specific commitments were made. And as evidenced over the past few years in Afghanistan and Libya, follow through on commitments is essential. Further, the United States and its Western partners need to proactively manage the dangers posed by European and American citizens now fighting alongside ISIS. The United States should work with its transatlantic partners and traditional allies to:

- **Enable reliable and capable partners in the region to take the fight directly to ISIS.** The United States is providing the greatest support to forces fighting ISIS. NATO and other U.S. allies should together develop a strategy to help the region counter ISIS with technical support and military assistance. This should include specific commitments to provide support to the Iraqi government, Kurdish forces, and third-way opposition alternatives to the Assad regime and ISIS in Syria.

- **Enhance law enforcement and intelligence fusion efforts to identify and counter ISIS and other terrorist fighters holding Western passports.** This should build on existing U.S.-European efforts in coordination with the International Criminal Police Organization, or INTERPOL. More than 12,000 foreign fighters are estimated to have flocked to Iraq and Syria. According to intelligence agencies and outside experts, one-quarter of these fighters come from Western countries. With an estimated 3,000 individuals, including perhaps 500 each from Britain and France, the dangers of extremists coming home to continue the fight with acts of terrorism cannot be ignored. Western countries should partner with allies in the Middle East and local communities on counter-radicalization efforts.

ENGAGEMENT AT THE UNITED NATIONS

The Obama administration has taken important steps to build international mechanisms on counterterrorism and should expand efforts at the United Nations during the upcoming U.N. General Assembly. This summer, the U.N. Security Council voted to add ISIS members to the Al Qaeda sanctions regime and invoked Chapter VII of the U.N. Charter, underscoring the threat that ISIS poses to international peace and security. This can serve as a useful basis for coordinating international action to disrupt ISIS's financing and other support. Given the divisions among leading global powers, action through the United Nations to authorize the use of force against ISIS, particularly in Syria, would prove difficult. Nonetheless, engagement through the United Nations can build political capital and legitimacy for unified international action against ISIS, including military strikes should they prove necessary. As part of this effort, the United States should:

- **Seek passage of a new U.N. Security Council resolution on foreign terrorist fighters.** The U.N. Security Council meeting that President Obama will personally chair later this month offers a unique opportunity to mobilize international action on the foreign terrorist fighter issue. A new U.N. Security Council resolution, or UNSCR, could sharpen countries' tools to counter radicalization and to meet their obligations to suppress terrorism and prevent terrorist recruitment. President Obama can stress that a new resolution should increase cooperation between various counterterrorism and law-enforcement bodies, helping frontline states track and coordinate with entities such as INTERPOL.

- **Urge the appointment of a U.N. special envoy to lead the international response to the regional humanitarian crisis and step up assistance for displaced Syrians and Iraqis.** During the U.N. General Assembly, the United States should support funding for United Nations' existing appeals for refugees in the region. U.S. leaders should call on U.N. Secretary General Ban ki-Moon to appoint a high-profile U.N. envoy to lead multilateral and bilateral relief efforts. This would not be a political position but rather modeled on the East Asia tsunami and Haiti earthquake relief efforts and focused on rallying global support for people affected by conflict and displaced throughout the region.
- **Encourage planning for a possible peacekeeping or stabilization mission.** The United States should begin discussions in the U.N. Security Council about planning for international peacekeepers in parts of Syria and perhaps Iraq after stability is restored. The mission could be modeled on the U.N. Interim Force in Lebanon, or UNIFIL, and draw on the lessons of a new generation of peace-

keeping operations currently underway in Mali and
the Democratic Republic of Congo.

PILLAR II: INCREASING SUPPORT FOR IRAQ

The Obama administration has established a coherent
framework for dealing with the security threats posed by
ISIS in Iraq and for advancing long-term stability in the
country. With a new, inclusive Iraqi government in place,
there are several key actions the United States should
take in the coming months on Iraq, including:

Political and diplomatic engagement

- **Re-engage the Iraqi government on an enduring U.S.-
Iraqi Strategic Framework Agreement**. A comprehensive agreement between the U.S. and Iraqi
governments that outlines broad areas of cooperation in the bilateral relationship will be crucial to any
long-term effort to support the Iraqi government in
re-establishing security in the country and countering
extremist groups such as ISIS.
- **Continue to condition U.S. military support on inclusive governance and Sunni outreach.** The successful
formation of a power-sharing government in Iraq on
September 8 may allow the United States to provide
greater security assistance to Iraq. Military action
without effective Sunni outreach risks increasing
support for ISIS and further inflaming the Sunni
community. The United States should continue to
offer support for a new, inclusive government under
Prime Minister Abadi and hold the new Iraqi government to a high standard of inclusion as a condition for
ongoing support.

- **Engage the Sunni tribes with our regional partners.** The United States should work with our regional Sunni partners in Jordan and the Gulf states to undertake outreach to the Sunni tribes in western Iraq. Any effort to re-engineer a program similar to the Sons of Iraq program—the U.S. military-led effort to combat Al Qaeda in Iraq by partnering with local Sunni tribes—as part of Baghdad's Sunni outreach can only be done effectively in cooperation with regional partners, particularly Saudi Arabia and Jordan. The United States should consider providing military and nonmilitary support to select tribes if they prove willing to take on ISIS.

Security assistance
- **Maintain conditional U.S. military support to the Iraqi Army.** If political outreach bears fruit, the United States should provide a robust support package to help the Iraqi Army move against ISIS, including air support. The United States can help restructure Iraqi national security institutions and help them rebuild the diverse elements of the Iraqi security forces that were dismantled under former Prime Minister Nouri al-Maliki. This can include the recruitment of local units to secure Sunni areas. It should encourage a new Iraqi government to include Sunni and Kurdish members in the senior ranks of Iraq's national security forces.
- **Re-enforce the Kurdistan Regional Government.** Bolster the Kurdish forces, known as the Peshmerga, to conduct limited offensive operations to force ISIS into a defensive position in northern Iraq. If

Sunni outreach from Baghdad is forthcoming, the U.S.
could support the Peshmerga in undertaking a coordinated campaign with the Iraqi Army.

Direct U.S. military action

- **Continue targeted strikes and intelligence, surveil-
lance, and reconnaissance support.** The United
States should remain engaged with the Iraqi national
security forces and other Iraqi forces such as the
Peshmerga to target ISIS and re-establish control of
Iraqi territory by legitimate Iraqi institutions.

PILLAR III: CONFRONTING ISIS IN SYRIA

The imperative of removing President Assad from power
must give way to the more immediate danger of ISIS
sanctuary. This does not mean partnering with President
Assad, who would likely continue to accommodate ISIS
and other extremists in order to keep his regime alive. The
United States will need to develop a shared understanding with Jordan, Lebanon, Turkey, and the members of the
Gulf Cooperation Council that countering ISIS is the first
priority as it takes the following steps:

Support for local actors

- **Strengthen the third-way Syrian opposition.** The
Obama administration proposed $500 million of
additional assistance to the Syrian opposition in
June. Congress should approve this request, and
the United States should accelerate efforts to build
up moderate opposition forces in Syria to combat
ISIS. New assistance should be directed to those
groups already receiving U.S. support, such as
Harakat Hazm and the Syrian Revolutionaries'

Front. Although these armed moderates have limited capabilities, new assistance could help them slow ISIS's advances and, over time, begin to reverse ISIS gains. The main short-term objective is to ensure that third-way anti-Assad and anti-ISIS forces survive. This effort will need to be coordinated with other regional partners that are able to support the armed opposition.

- **Expand outreach to Sunni tribes in Syria.** The United States should expand its outreach to include Sunni tribes as a means to limit ISIS's influence. ISIS's use of foreign fighters to govern will undercut the influence of the traditional tribal structure over time. The United States should establish common cause with Sunni tribal leaders and give those willing to stand against ISIS the support needed to provide for their constituents.

Political transition

- **Maintain the long-term objective of transition from the Assad regime in Syria.** Efforts to strengthen the regional offensive against ISIS will not succeed if these actions are seen in the region as directly benefiting the Assad regime. The United States should continue to work with regional actors to explore and exploit fissures within the Assad government's ruling elite. Such fissures could open up more viable pathways toward a political transition from President Assad.
- **Rebuild the regional and international foundations to mediate a solution to the Syrian conflict.** Although peace talks in Geneva failed in early 2014, the efforts outlined in this report—

including increased support for third-way opposition alternatives to the Assad regime and ISIS—could set the conditions for a political transition in Syria. U.S. diplomats should work to reinvigorate a regional contact group on the Syrian conflict to start building a foundation for new peace talks. Ultimately, the conflict in Syria requires a political solution.

- **Possible targeted airstrikes again ISIS Consider expanding airstrikes into Syria in coalition with Gulf partners and NATO.** As in Iraq, airpower may be a critical element of disrupting ISIS in Syria and supporting the moderate opposition. Any strikes within Syria should be conducted in coalition with America's Gulf partners and NATO allies, ideally with U.N. support. Airstrikes may be employed to support third-way opposition fighters as they take the fight to ISIS, as well as to defend these opposition fighters against attacks from Assad's security forces. Robust intelligence collection should precede such strikes. The United States should, of course, reserve the right to undertake unilateral military action if the ISIS threat becomes imminent to the United States as has been the case with Al Qaeda in Yemen or al-Shabaab in Somalia. In light of what is likely to be sustained effort, President Obama and congressional leaders should cooperate to develop an appropriate authorization for military action against ISIS that can help pave the way to a durable framework for fighting terrorism.

CONCLUSION

ISIS control of large swaths of territory in Iraq and Syria poses a clear threat to American interests and to stability across the Middle East. If unchecked, ISIS's brutality, growing capacity, and recruitment of foreign fighters can significantly increase the risks of international terrorism. The United States can meet this threat in coalition with its allies and partners, but all involved parties must be prepared to pull their weight. ISIS can only be defeated by determined action from an international and regional coalition in which a broad range of countries decide that enough is enough and commit to a joint effort. U.S. leadership and engagement will be essential to the success of such an effort, which represents an opportunity to help bring greater stability to the region as a whole.

1. The authors of the above article recommend that US military engagement against ISIS be limited to airstrikes. They also call for other measures such as greater intelligence efforts, international diplomacy, and outreach to local tribes. But is the general approach they outline for dealing with the threat of ISIS specific and forceful enough?

2. Since this article was published, ISIS has conducted several high profile acts of terror, most notably the attacks in Paris in November 2015. Do you think this makes the positions above too moderate and possibly obsolete? Or are these strategies still generally applicable?

"THE GOOD COUNTRY," BY TIM KANE, FROM *COMMENTARY*, DECEMBER 1, 2014

President Obama's foreign policy of disengagement has been shattered by the events of the past year. His conviction that a retrenched United States would be better for Americans at home and for people around the globe has only invited aggression, from the Middle East to Europe to the Pacific. The animating ideas behind Obama's policies have been called into question: the beliefs that "military solutions" are always inferior, that American troop deployments are tantamount to occupations, that multilateral compromise is more moral than decisive unilateral action, and that America's enforcement of world order does more harm than good.

Obama is actively uncomfortable exercising American power abroad, but he is entirely comfortable exercising centralized power at home. He believes that a strong central government is a moral force inside the United States, but he does not believe that American power is a force for good outside our borders. He is especially certain that American "boots on the ground" don't do anyone any good—not us and not the countries to which they are deployed.

This is wrong. Indeed, it is tragically wrong. Having compared growth and development indicators across all countries of the world against a database of U.S. "boots on the ground" since 1950, I've discovered a stunning truth: In country after country, prosperity—in the form of economic growth and human development—has emerged where American soldiers have trod.

Unique among dominant powers in world history, America intervenes in the world not merely to advance its own narrow interests but to forward a greater good. And that is due in large measure to the belief that the greater good is in America's national interest—that a freer and more prosperous world is one in which the United States will flourish. After the Second World War, the United States established "what we might call a global economic and security commons," in the words of former Secretary of State George Shultz. Billions of poor people experienced economic development thanks to their own efforts—and thanks to the Pax Americana that enabled them to do so. Without America, world economic output would not have grown from $5.1 trillion to $70.2 trillion in 70 years. World population would not have quintupled after 1950. And child mortality would not have been cut by two-thirds.

Critics call it empire. Academics call it hegemony. Some of its champions have called it unipolarity. But the data show a distinguishing feature beyond those descriptions: The projection of universal liberty has been the beating heart of U.S. foreign policy. But not for this president. At West Point earlier this year, Obama declared: "To say that we have an interest in pursuing peace and freedom beyond our borders is not to say that every problem has a military solution.... U.S. military action cannot be the only—or even primary—component of our leadership in every instance. Just because we have the best hammer does not mean that every problem is a nail."

Our power is a "hammer"—in his view, a destructive tool. But is that really what a hammer is? Hammers are tools for construction, not destruction. In that sense, the metaphor works very well. Indeed, from 1950 to 2010, more than 30 million U.S. troops were deployed around the world, the vast majority to allied countries, stationed in permanent bases, and cooperating in peace. They were building, not destroying.

The cases involving sustained military intervention get all the attention, but they are exceptions to the rule. Critics who focus on them see the scale of America's global footprint, but they do not see the scope.

In a typical year over the past half-century, 19 countries hosted more than a thousand American soldiers. Japan, Korea, and Germany are the best known hosts of American military bases, but most people are unaware that U.S. soldiers lived in Bosnia, the Philippines, and Italy (host to 10,000 U.S. troops per year for more than 60 years).

American troop deployments overseas from 1950 to 1989 (the Cold War era) averaged 610,453 per year. During the "peace dividend" decade that followed, the total force strength shrank by two-fifths, from 2.5 to 1.6 million (then shrank again in the most recent decade to 1.4 million). Boots on foreign ground declined abruptly in the decade after 1990 to only 258,709 before rising again to 357,236 between the years 2002 and 2012.

Contrary to conventional wisdom, most troop deployments were not to countries at war—the sole exception being the years from 1966 to 1970, the height of the war in Vietnam. In the 1980s, 300,000 American forces were stationed in European allied countries, 100,000 in Asian allied countries, 5,000 in Turkey (a NATO ally), and 9,000 in Panama.

What happened in the places where American military personnel put down roots is nothing short of astonishing. The most dramatic stories are, of course, those of Germany and Japan, which the United States cultivated into financial superpowers after they had been crushed in the war. The most remarkable story is South Korea's. Average per capita income in South Korea climbed from $1,500 in 1953 to $27,000 in 2013. The U.S.-allied South was much poorer than the Stalinist North, and autocratic rule was the norm for decades—but in the long run, economic freedom led to breathtaking prosperity and, later, a robust liberal democracy. Credit goes to the South Koreans, to be sure, but its American alliance, the provision of an authentic security umbrella, and tens of thousands of Americans on the ground prepared the way to a better future.

Statistical analysis reveals that countries allied with the United States flourished while other countries did not. One startling finding in a study I conducted with Garett Jones of George Mason University is that countries hosting more American forces experienced much faster economic growth than their peers—roughly 1 percentage point per year. And that's after accounting for all the other variables that matter for growth.

This is no small claim. Economists have studied the factors associated with economic growth perhaps more intensely than any other question. So when a new variable is proposed, it must pass robustness tests. This one has, by maintaining statistical significance in explaining growth when hundreds of other variable combinations are considered as well (such as the starting level of GDP), and also where high-growth outliers such as Korea, Japan, and Germany are not included. American troop deployments, across hundreds of regressions, proved statistically and economically significant.

A second example: non-economic development. It turns out that allied countries with a greater U.S. troop presence experienced better outcomes on measures of life expectancy and children's mortality. This effect held even for countries growing at the same rate. Furthermore, it held during two distinct eras, pre- and post-1990. Life expectancy worldwide increased by 10 years between 1970 and the present. But it improved more quickly in countries that hosted American troops, and more slowly elsewhere. The worldwide mortality rate of children dropped from 132 to 55 per 1,000 live births during the same period, but again, the results were better among America's allies. Statistical tests show that a tenfold increase of U.S. troops during a 20-year period in a typical country improved the reduction in children's mortality by 2.2 percentage points and improved life expectancy gains by 1 percentage point. (One factor, interestingly enough, was an increased number of telephone lines in countries with a heavy U.S. troop presence, which ensured connections between rural communities, health-care workers, and supplies that extend lives.) These relationships are statistically significant, even when controlling for initial GDP per capita, conflict, and economic aid. American troops made the difference.

These results are not due to the fact that an American military presence provides more dollars to the host countries. The effect of American deployments seems to be nonlinear—meaning that each additional soldier has a decreasingly positive impact. The correlation between economic growth in a country and the number of U.S. troops stationed there is 0.20, and it is even lower for troops per capita, but the correlation between growth and the log of troops is 0.49. That means that an increase of one order of magnitude—whether it's 50 to 500 GIs or 100,000 to 1 million—has the same effect.

From this we can infer that the presence of U.S. troops is less about "nation-building" in terms of Keynesian stimulus and more about ideas—the spread of notions such as property rights, investment security, and rule of law.

The means by which troops enhance growth and human development are not fully understood, but one channel is surely the effective deterrence of interstate violence. Harvard University psychologist Steven Pinker has drawn attention to the dramatic reduction in war deaths since 1945. This "Long Peace" was initially credited to the bipolar standoff during the Cold War that prevented brushfire wars across the globe. But even after the fall of the Berlin Wall, deaths due to interstate and even civil wars continued to decline. The data demonstrating that American troops are a source of economic, political, and life-enhancing betterment are real, global, and durable over many decades. This is not a theoretical construct. And properly understood, the finding can help America shape better strategic engagement in the future.

Note here that I am not talking about the times America has staged emergency interventions for humanitarian reasons—the case in which our "good nation" behavior is most immediately apparent. In early January 2010, a massive earthquake in Haiti displaced millions and nearly collapsed the government there. Within days, the U.S. Air Force had opened the main airport and was managing more than 100 inbound aid flights daily. Over 13,000 military personnel were rapidly deployed that month to Haiti. In 2004, one of the largest earthquakes ever recorded created a tsunami in the Indian Ocean and was followed by a global disaster-relief effort led by the Navy as well as nearly a thousand relief flights by Air Force cargo aircraft.

The standard way to discuss foreign policy is in terms of how it serves the national interest—the maintenance of commercial interests abroad, the protection of nationals in other countries, and as a check against the ambitions of others. But time and again, conventional definitions of national interest are insufficient when it comes to capturing the impetus and drive for American action outside our borders. In 1999, Bill Clinton did not conduct a 48-day air war over Kosovo to boost the stock price of Lockheed Martin or to protect American access to mineral deposits. He did so to prevent a genocide on the European continent, partly out of a national feeling of shame that we had done little to prevent the genocide that took place in Rwanda a few years earlier. In this way, as in many others, America's foreign policy transcends the classic understanding of national interest as it has been understood since the European powers signed the Treaty of Westphalia in 1648.

It then follows to ask, is this transcendent foreign policy good or bad for the United States? In the wake of the Iraq War's unpopularity, the answer for many is no: "If the history of the past 20 years teaches us anything," Harvard's Stephen Walt has written, "it is that forceful American interference of this sort just makes these problems worse." Realists like Walt are disquieted by any principle of international engagement based on something more than narrow and naked self-interest. They dislike the impetus for "meddling" and "adventurism" and prefer the constrained vision of John Quincy Adams by which America "goes not abroad, in search of monsters to destroy."

The realists are not the only objectors. More important, perhaps, are those on the left and the far right who believe America's transcendent foreign policy is immoral, and that we are acting not on behalf of good but on behalf of an imperialist ideology of vague but offensive provenance. For them, American foreign policy is characterized by disgusting staged photos of prisoners in an Iraqi jail on a single night, or a single massacre carried out by a small platoon in a Vietnamese village in 1968 at a time when a half million Americans were in that country, or by support for unsavory dictators at various points over the past 70 years. In this view, our power has made us monstrous.

Another common objection to a robust American military presence in the world is that it is financially unsustainable, especially in our current economic state. There is steady support for belt-tightening, and concerns about budgetary excess exist even beyond the Tea Party and traditional budget hawks. In October, Gallup polling found that three out of every four voters considered the federal deficit very important. And yet, earlier in the year, Gallup also found "no broad consensus among Americans that the U.S. is spending too much or too little on the military." This suggests that the deep national concern about federal spending does not apply in the same way to the military.

The reason for that is simple: The argument that America's military spending is a fiscal train-wreck waiting to happen is simply not true. Even proponents of reducing military expenditures admit as much. In a 2012 paper for the libertarian (and markedly anti-interventionist) Cato Institute, two scholars acknowledged that "foolish" U.S. military-spending patterns were in fact "sustainable."

The reality is that U.S. defense expenditures have declined from 9-10 percent of GDP in the 1950s and '60s to 6 percent in the 70s and '80s to 4 percent in recent decades. What's unsustainable is not the budget, apparently, but the willpower to stay engaged. As Justin Logan and Benjamin H. Friedman wrote: "That such a small slice of American wealth accounts for nearly half the world's military spending shows how cheap military hegemony has become for Americans."

Perhaps it is this common characterization of Pax Americana as a hegemony that we need to examine. If we approach the historical record with care, we can see that the American story since the Second World War is hardly imperial, nor is it a story of hegemony. It is something new under the sun. U.S. military interventions have come, in all cases, in situations with limited benefit to the American bottom line. There was no material advantage to saving South Korea, a bloody and costly war that ended well. And there was nothing to be exploited in Vietnam, an even bloodier and more costly war that ended badly. In these cases, America was determined to counter Communist aggression, and not merely for its own citizens. As Ronald Reagan said in the famous "A Time for Choosing" speech 50 years ago, "We cannot buy our security, our freedom from the threat of the bomb, by committing an immorality so great as saying to a billion human beings now enslaved behind the Iron Curtain, 'Give up your dreams of freedom because to save our own skins, we're willing to make a deal with your slave masters.'" America's presidents and her soldiers were willing to make selfless sacrifices for the liberty of others. This is not hegemony.

I would suggest that the unlearned lesson of the Cold War is not that Communism was contained but that Communism was outgrown. The prosperity created through free-market development in American-allied countries stood in sharp contrast with the slower growth in centrally planned neighboring economies. West Germany outgrew the East, and everyone knew it. Beijing eventually changed course when the success of capitalism in Tokyo, Seoul, Singapore, and Hong Kong could no longer be denied. (In one of the key moments before he announced the policy of perestroika, Mikhail Gorbachev famously went on a tour of a Canadian agribusiness, asked how many workers it took to harvest the fields, and was told, to his shock and shame: none.)

For 40 years, the United States enforced global peace through strength. Following the posture of calm leadership established by President Dwight Eisenhower in the 1950s, the Cold War was called cold because the confrontation never broke into direct hostilities. We nurtured our allies and waited. It is said that good fences make good neighbors, but in a global neighborhood of crumbling fences, it will be good neighbors that win over old enemies. Countries that profit from American values have no need to ally with an oppressive Moscow or Beijing against the United States. Rather, they share our interest in protecting a free and prosperous global order, and serve as bastions of stability and opportunity. This approach resulted in important bilateral security agreements with Japan, South Korea, Australia, and other countries where American troops have left their mark. It's tempting to criticize what foreign-policy analyst Michael Mandelbaum has called "foreign policy as social work," but few among us would prefer to live in a world untouched by American beneficence.

What lessons can we draw from this? How can this Good Country shape the 21st century? A long, patient commitment to engaging with allies across the spectrum of hard and soft power is one obvious bedrock value we must uphold to expand the "peace and security commons" for the next generation. Understanding that there may be little short-term national interest in investing time and treasure in Africa should not dissuade us. But setting aside the controversial role of America in nurturing freedom and democracy, we should recognize the simple calculus of forward deployment of U.S. armed forces in hot spots before they boil over. The Baltics are a top priority, followed closely by a focus on the Philippines and others in the South Pacific (some of this is under way in Australia). A case can be made that engaging more directly in both Central and South America will help turn around the developmental stagnation of the past decade.

It would be a mistake to read the evidence about the positive impact of troop deployments as a clarion call for, simply, more. Indeed, that is the confused, instinctive reaction of many to the empirical reality of the troops' effect. Let's think about this from the economist's perspective of supply and demand. A strategy of pushing troops to poor, unstable countries is not the way this policy works. Rather, the history of seven decades of hard-power engagement shows that the United States respected the "demand side" of the relationship. When France in the 1960s and the Philippines in the 1990s wanted U.S. forces out, out they went. The troops' effect is empirically positive precisely because recent history is dominated by allies such as South Korea and Japan and dozens of other nations that wanted and still want forward deployments of U.S. troops. Indeed, the biggest mistake is for a president to get caught up in seeking out and hammering enemies, because the U.S. military is arguably the softest power at its disposal.

And what of the Middle East? Ask yourself: Which nations in the Middle East are true allies? Israel, to be sure. Others are treated more as acquaintances. The public never hears the president talk about Jordan, Kuwait, Turkey, or Egypt the way that Cold War presidents talked about Korea, Japan, Germany, France, Italy, the Philippines, Thailand, Turkey, and Taiwan, just to name a few. Supporting allies should be our priority when it comes to engagement. Focus on the positive, constructive engagement first, and let our shared interests guide the fighting, together.

But given the realities of the Middle East, pinning America's engagement strategy on Israel (population: 8 million) is the equivalent of pinning the Cold War effort in Europe from 1945 to 1989 on a single alliance with Belgium (population: 11 million). Supporting the one true democracy in the Middle East is paramount, but it is not enough.

Where are Air Force, Army, Marine, and Naval bases welcomed? Where are American soldiers allowed and encouraged to mix and mingle and marry? When troops are deployed to Asia, their assignments are long and the bases are open. By contrast, tours of duty in the Middle East are short, in bases that are secreted bubbles. These things matter. We will know the "good country effect" is taking place when American troops in the Middle East no longer live like astronauts on a moon colony but rather co-exist with the people they are there to defend and help.

The tangle of relationships among Middle Eastern states (and non-states) is complex and fragile, you might say. Was it any different in 1950s Asia, where our closest allies in Tokyo, Seoul, and Manila had been bitter enemies? The complexities in 1960s Indochina or the Balkans in the 1990s rival our era as well. The bottom line is that America's engagement has been successful even when its war record is mixed, and the successes point to a strategy of strong support for our allies, cultural and economic openness, investing in human development, and above all—patience.

1. The author claims "America intervenes in the world not merely to advance its own narrow interests but to forward a greater good." Do you agree with this statement? Why or why not?

2. Did you read this article as merely an apology for self-serving US imperialism? Or does it present a valid and objective critique of our current "intervention exhaustion"—coming after a decade of ineffectual presence in Iraq and Afghanistan?

"THE LEFT'S FALSE LOGIC ON SYRIA," BY STANLEY HELLER, FROM *SOCIALIST WORKER*, MARCH 1, 2016

In the war in Syria, much of the left is falling for the classic false logic of "the enemy of my enemy is my friend."

The thinking is that since the U.S. government and "the West" are now opposing Russia's military intervention in Syria, among other conflicts, and they have long threatened Iran and other nations and forces that are part of the Shia bloc in the Middle East, these opponents of the U.S. must be the "good guys," or at least the "lesser evils."

It's a mistake. All the blocs are murderous and enemies of humanity. For left writers and journalists like Patrick Cockburn, Stephen Cohen and Robert Fisk to join the right-wing *National Review* and liberals like Steven Kinzer in cheering on Assad and Putin's conquests is awful. Actually, more than that, it is a calamity.

Now, since I will be accused of being naïve at best and neo-con slime at worst, I'll mention some my anti-imperialist bona fides: marching against the Vietnam war; arrested over South Africa; arrested over Nicaragua; arrested for yelling at George H.W. Bush about the hundreds of thousands he killed with sanctions in Iraq; and a demonstrator against the threatened U.S.-Israel war against Iran. As leader of the Middle East Crisis Committee in Connecticut, I also opposed Barack Obama's desire to bomb Syria in 2013. And there's the 33 years I've been working for Palestinian rights.

Now let's talk about the Islamic State—not the Islamic State in Iraq and Syria (ISIS), but the Islamic State of Iran (ISI).

It was completely right to oppose a U.S.-Israeli war on Iran. Iran was no danger to the U.S., nor an "existential" threat to Israel. However, one antiwar graphic commonly used to defend Iran at that time was misleading. It showed around 50 countries that the U.S. had attacked or sabotaged since the Second World War, and compared that record to Iran, which supposedly had zero victims on its list.

But that was wrong. The Iranian regime has for years been involved in attacking the people of Syria.

Iran's support for Assad is enormous. As Eli Lake wrote in a Bloomberg View column: "[A] spokeswoman for the UN special envoy for Syria, Staffan de Mistura, told me that the envoy estimates Iran spends $6 billion annually on Assad's government. Other experts I spoke to put the number even higher."

Last November the Pentagon estimated that Iran had 2,000 of its own troops in Syria, but that's just for starters. There's also Hezbollah, the Lebanese militia, which has 6,000 to 8,000 fighters in Syria. Hezbollah is very close to Iran, if not completely an Islamic State of Iran asset. Its fighters are a key part of the sieges of Madaya and Moadamiyeh, which are causing scores to drop dead of starvation. There are also Iraqi Shia militias in Syria undoubtedly supported by Iran, along with undocumented Afghans living in Iran who have been recruited to fight in Syria.

Iran and its allies are participating in an immense crime. Back in 2014, Michael Karadjis summarized the Assad regime's behavior in this way: "Assad has pretty much leveled every city in Syria, turned the whole country to rubble, killed over 100,000 people to be generous, tortured tens of thousands to death in medieval dungeons, bombed hospitals and schools with a fury rivaling the Zionist regime in Gaza, and at that very time, last August, had bombed hundreds of children in their sleep with chemical weapons."

That pretty much summed up the record then, but we need to add the regime's use of barrel bombs and its starvation sieges of hundreds of thousands of people since then. Until it stopped counting, the UN estimate 250,000 dead in the massacres and fighting, but recently, the Syrian Center for Policy Research issued a report saying that 470,000 Syrians have been killed.

Overwhelmingly, these people have been slaughtered by the Assad-Iran-Russia Triple Alliance. Free Syrian Army and Islamist forces don't have an air force or anything like the weaponry available to Assad and his friends. Even journalist Patrick Cockburn, who sees Assad as a lesser evil, admits that contested areas are "systematically bombarded by government aircraft and artillery, making them uninhabitable."

Among the victims are the people killed slowly in Assad's prisons. A United Nations report released on February 3 detailed "deaths on a massive scale" in Assad government facilities. It concluded, "There are reasonable grounds to believe that the conduct described amounts to extermination as a crime against humanity."

There's no reason to doubt the UN findings. They repeat what was shown in the thousands of photographs brought to Britain by defecting the Syrian army photographer "Caesar." That Iran would ally with the brutal Assad gang should not be a huge surprise. Remember how the ISI came into being: In 1978 and '79, mass demonstrations often led by Marxist parties stayed out in the streets in Iran despite fearsome repression by the U.S.-backed regime. In the end, former guerrillas overwhelmed the Shah's guards, and the "Shah of Shahs" ran away.

Ayatollah Khomeini promised an Islamic revolution, a rejection of Western control and social justice without socialism. Within a month, he was showing what he meant by "revolution." The wearing of the hijab by women was made compulsory in all government and public offices, and the crudest repression was unleashed. The left was destroyed, and thousands of people were imprisoned. "[S]ummary execution of political prisoners became common practice," according to Index on Censorship. There were waves of executions, with the worst coming at the end of the Iran-Iraq War during the 1980s. "As the war ended, the government killed around 15,000 socialists, communists and members of the Mujahedin who were in prison," the Index on Censorship reported.

The Iranian regime still has a taste for execution. Last July, Amnesty International estimated that there had been almost 700 executions in Iran in just the first six moths of the year. This is far more than the 158 killed by the head-choppers of Saudi Arabia.

On February 15, a Doctors Without Borders hospital was blown up in the northwestern town of Maarat al-Numan. Unlike a similar hospital in Kunduz, Afghanistan, which was demolished by a U.S. air strike, the staff at this Syrian hospital had *not* given its GPS coordinates to the Syrian government. The reason is that the staff thought, given the record of Assad and Russian attacks on health facilities, they would be safer if they refused to coordinate with the Assad government.

According to Physicians for Human Rights, 240 health clinics have been bombed and 700 doctors and health workers killed in Syria, overwhelmingly by Assad forces.

Many of you will have seen the video from a Russian drone company showing the complete destruction of Homs, once a city of 600,000 people. There, too, should be no surprise. Putin's first "success" was his brutal victory in the second war on Chechnya, which the U.S. group Solidarity aptly called a "near-genocidal war."

Russia today is tyranny with a fig leaf of elections to try to provide legitimacy. Dissidents are murdered in the streets. Former Deputy Prime Minister Boris Nemtsov was shot to death in view of the Kremlin. Alexander Litvenenko was poisoned to death by radioactive polonium, and there have been many other political assassinations. Psychiatric punishment, like during the Soviet era, is back in vogue.

Oh, I "demonized" Putin. No apologies—his regime is an appalling capitalist kleptocracy. If his behavior inside Russia isn't revealing enough, consider the warm relations and military coordination between Russia and Israel. Then talk about lesser evils.

Russia has sold the Assad dynasty all manner of weapons for decades, and now, with its nonstop bombing, it may be the main killing force in Syria. The *Washington Post* reports that under a secret treaty with the government, "Russian military personnel and shipments can pass in and out of Syria at will, and aren't subject to controls by Syrian authorities...Syrians can't enter Russian bases without Russia's permission. " It's a classic colonial relationship.

What are other historical analogies here? I'm thinking that the closest one is Spain in the 1930s. One side is willing to use unlimited amounts of violence and is overwhelming supported by tyrannical outside forces. In Spain, it was

Franco's fascists, supported by Hitler and Mussolini. Here, it's Assad backed by Russia and Iran.

In the 1930s, the Popular Front of liberals, revolutionaries and the Communist Party fought gamely, supported weakly by the Soviet Union. In Syria, revolutionaries (to hell with the term "moderates") and Islamists, including political reactionaries. Sure there are differences. In Spain, the left was "the government"—in Syria, the Assad dynasty is "the government." So what? The defeat of democratic forces in Spain was catastrophic. Think appeasement and the Second World War.

Obviously, this is just an analogy, with many differences between then and now. But if Aleppo is starved and bombed into submission, it's very possible Assad may succeed in retaking most or all of Syria, and that, too, will be catastrophic. There will be massive numbers of new refugees and a worldwide increase in the appeal of ISIS and al-Qaeda to Sunni Muslims. There will be a rightist frenzy in the U.S. about who "lost" Syria and demands for ever-tougher military actions toward Russia and Iran, with all the risks of a major war. And much of the left will have been disgraced by standing by and watching, or even applauding the process.

So what should the left be doing instead?

First, I want to deal with one argument that goes something like this: "The main enemy is at home. I have to pay taxes that support U.S. imperialism—that should be my main concern."

I agree up to a point. Certainly, you deal with things that are your personal responsibility, and of course, over the last two decades, "the West" has done much more killing than "the East." The million or so slain by sanctions against Iraq by the Bushes and Clintons is far larger than the number killed by Russia and Iran in Syria, at least so far. So, yes, we oppose U.S. wars in every way that we can.

But increasingly, "the main enemy" reasoning is being used to mean that the *only* thing we should deal with is U.S. government interventions and crimes. That's so screwed up. It's a betrayal of people who are or should be our friends. It's also supremely foolish to think secondary enemies can't be deadly, too. Lesser evil can still be monstrous.

So what concrete things should the left be demanding and doing? We should follow the playbook of the boycott, divestment and sanctions campaign that Palestinian activists have devised.

First off, we must demand the breaking of the sieges. An incredible number of people are under siege in Syria. Back in January, pictures of people in skeletal condition in Madaya went viral, but that's just scratching the surface. There's something like a million people living under siege in Syria. It's a war crime and was specifically forbidden by the United Nations Security Council in 2014.

We should call for the UN (and if that fails, the U.S.), to defy the sieges and start airdrops of humanitarian relief. CODEPINK has a petition to that effect with over 2,000 signers. British efforts have been even more successful, getting over 60,000 signers. Food convoys are obviously a better way to send in aid. The U.N. should send them without asking for "permission" from Assad forces.

Second, demonstrate in public, in front of Russian or Iranian consulates or embassies, and at speaking events. The goal should be to expose and shame them—and we should bring signs about U.S. and Saudis outrages to discourage attendance by rightists.

Third, refuse to appear on Russian or Iranian television. It's shocking that people on the left would accept employment on Iran's Press TV or Putin's Russia Today. Even answering their press queries is debatable.

Fourth, boycott Russian and Iranian goods. I know the U.S. government is just now ending its sanctions on Iran—sanctions that were deadly in their impact. I'm not talking about that. I'm advocating a people's boycott of companies and persons connected to the regimes. Just as we do with Palestine, make lists of products and companies, and peacefully but loudly harass them.

Fifth, correct the narrative being spread by pro-Assad writers. There should be a total U.S. break with the Saudi "Kingdom of Horrors"—but increasingly, we're hearing a liberal-left narrative that says the Saudis started the violence in Syria, in coordination with the U.S. Actually, the Saudis didn't even publicly criticize Assad until six months after the start of the popular uprising in 2011.

True, Saudi Arabia has funded jihadis, among other militias, but the Saudis and the U.S. are only the number-three culprit in creating the Syrian disaster. Assad is clearly number one, and his allies are number two.

Sixth, oppose any U.S.-Russian dictated settlement for Syria. No to forcing an Assad-led "coalition" government onto Syria. All of the imperial and regional powers should butt out and stick to humanitarian work.

Is it too late for Syria? A big BDS campaign takes years to get going, but the start of a serious effort will be noticed immediately by Russia and Iran. It could change their behavior.

And even if they won't stop their assault and Aleppo does fall, it will not be over, just like the cause of Spain was never really extinguished. It lived on in guerrilla actions and workers' struggles until the Franco regime was brought down.

As the left cried out in Spain: "No pasaran!" They shall not pass.

1. This article refrains from any geopolitical policy directives. Do you find this refreshing, or unhelpful?

2. How likely do you feel it is that regional players will stick to humanitarian work, as the author recommends?

CHAPTER 5

WHAT THE MEDIA SAY

Historically, a pro-Israeli bias has profoundly influenced US foreign policy in the Middle East. Though few wish to subvert our friendship with the only functional democracy in the region, America's special relationship with Israel has shaped its response to the Syrian conflict—arguably for the worse.

Israel would like nothing more than to see Assad go. As Morgan Duchesney reports, Israeli officials candidly admit they would prefer Al-Qaeda, or possibly even ISIS, in power over Assad in Syria. This is based on geopolitics specific to Israel, but has forced the US into a difficult spot: either cooperate with Russia, Iran, and Assad, or step up backing to rebel groups that are not trustworthy. Obama has tried to have it both ways, publicly denouncing Assad, while backing select opposition half-heartedly, as to not alienate the status quo.

The Western media is complicit in maintaining this confusing dynamic. It habitually depicts Palestinians as terrorists, but excuses disproportionate Israeli force as self-defense. Furthermore, corporate media has vilified Putin's backing of regional ally Assad, though this is no different than our position with respect to Israel. Finally, the press typically downplays that key players opposing Assad (other than ISIS) are extremists such as Al-Qaeda. Some suggest we have tried to rebrand jihadists as "moderates."

Meanwhile, ISIS has stepped up its media campaign with slick promotional videos and a sophisticated presence on Twitter. These recruitment tools are working, but how this will play out in Syria and Iraq remains to be seen.

"GAZA'S AGONY: AN ALTERNATIVE PERSPECTIVE ON RECENT EVENTS," BY MORGAN DUCHESNEY, FROM *HUMANIST PERSPECTIVES, SPRING 2015*

The struggle of people against power is the struggle of memory against forgetting. Milan Kundera

INTRODUCTION: HISTORICAL CONTEXT
MISSING FROM CORPORATE
MEDIA COVERAGE

The corporate media has largely ignored the brutal chronology of events in Gaza and the horrific living conditions that have gradually intensified since Israel officially left the territory in 2005. While the reasons for such blinkered journalism are beyond the scope of this article, I will offer an idea from Chomsky and Pappe for the reader's consideration: "... the imperial mentality is so deeply embedded in Western culture that this travesty passes without criticism, even notice." (1) Considering the current state of affairs in Gaza, this absence of depth and context creates the false impression that Palestinians are innately violent and self-destructive.

Former Israeli leader Ariel Sharon cynically agreed to abandon Gaza to the Palestinians in 2005, although the move was falsely presented to the world as a magnanimous gesture. As senior Sharon advisor Dov Weissglass said to a *Haaretz* reporter in a 2004 moment of candor typical of the Israeli press:

> The significance of the disengagement plan is the freezing of the peace process ... And when you freeze that process, you prevent the establishment of a Palestinian state, and you prevent a discussion on the refugees, the borders and Jerusalem. Effectively, this whole package called the Palestinian state, with all that it entails, has been removed from our agenda. (2)

Since Gaza's Palestinian leadership are aware of this attitude, their tendency to cynicism and mistrust in dealing with a peace partner so vastly superior in arms, finance and superpower backing is understandable.

The Western public needs more accurate information about the punitive conditions Gaza residents endure and how that might explain the rise of a brutal organization like Hamas. While little is said about the highly effective pre-1948 Jewish terrorism campaign in Palestine, reference to those past events might provide much-needed context for the current activities of Hamas and other Palestinian militant groups who attack Israel with futile tactics like suicide bombers, mortars and crude rockets. These attacks are consistently met with a devastatingly disproportionate Israeli response but the rocket attacks continue. The IDF (Israeli Defense Force) in 2008 adopted the brutal Dahiyya Doctrine, so named for the Shiite quarter of Beirut that was obliterated in a 2006 IDF air bombardment. In Chomsky and Pappe's words, the doctrine requires "... the comprehensive destruction of areas in their entirety and the employment of disproportional force in response to the launch of missiles." (3)

While the corporate media consistently condemns Hamas' refusal to recognize the legitimacy of the Israeli state, they ignore the fact that this refusal is mainly based on the reality that inherent in such recognition is abandonment of the Palestinian diaspora's right of return to their lost homes. On the other hand, "Israel's settlement and development programs in the occupied territories—all illegal, as Israel was informed in 1967

145

by its highest court and recently affirmed by the World Court—are designed to undermine the possibility of a viable Palestinian state." (4) In fact, Israel has seized so much of the West Bank and East Jerusalem that a Palestinian state will only be possible with a mass evacuation of Israelis, an unlikely event. While Hamas is often accused of wishing to destroy Israel, they certainly have little ability to accomplish such a goal.

CORPORATE MEDIA ASSUMPTIONS ABOUT THE CAUSE OF THE RECENT VIOLENCE IN GAZA

Canada's corporate media continue to provide propaganda services to the Israeli state by presenting recent events as a noble and measured Israeli response to the terrorists of Hamas. According to an August 22, 2014, Associated Press article in the *Globe and Mail*:

> ...the [Hamas]kidnapping of three Israeli teens while they were hitchhiking on June 12, along with the discovery of their bodies two weeks later, sparked a broad Israeli crackdown on Hamas members in the West Bank. Hamas responded with heavy rocket fire out of the Gaza strip, leading Israel to launch an aerial and ground invasion of the territory.

The July 21, 2014, issue of *Maclean's* magazine echoed this condemnation of Hamas by declaring, "Israel launched air strikes in the Gaza Strip in retaliation for Palestinian rocket attacks on Israeli towns; escalation seems inevitable..." In an editorial of

September 4, 2014, Sun Media offered the following critique of Liberal candidate and former Canadian general Andrew Leslie who dared hold the Israeli military accountable for civilian casualties in Gaza: "No mention that Hamas started the conflict by murdering three Israeli students. No mention that Hamas uses civilians as human shields when firing rockets at Israel, or that it tells civilians to ignore Israeli warnings of an imminent attack."

Both media outlets omitted the fact that Gaza is so crowded that it is nearly impossible to perform any military activity without some proximity to civilians. As for Israeli warnings, Gaza Palestinians have nowhere to hide as the bombs and missiles explode around them. Perhaps Hamas rocket attacks on Israel will be more acceptable if they adopt an Israeli-style early warning system.

ISRAELI VIOLATION OF 2012 CEASEFIRE AGREEMENT

Notably absent from the corporate media is any mention of the deeper reasons for the recent spate of Hamas rocket attacks. Contrary to corporate media reports, IDF began immediately violating the ceasefire agreement that followed Operation Pillar of Defense, the 2012 invasion of Gaza. In commenting on the violation, Noam Chomsky refers to the work of Nathan Thrall, senior Middle East analyst for the International Crisis Group:

Israeli intelligence recognized that Hamas was observing the terms of the ceasefire. "Israel,"

Thrall wrote, "therefore saw little incentive in
upholding its end of the deal. In the three months
following the ceasefire, its forces made regular
incursions into Gaza..." (5)

Therefore, when one considers those events, July
2014's Operation Protective Edge was almost inevitable,
as Chomsky notes:

The two major Palestinian groupings, Gaza-based
Hamas and the Fatah-dominated Palestinian
Authority in the West Bank signed a unity agreement. Finally, the unity government accepted the
three conditions that Washington and the European Union had long demanded: non-violence,
adherence to past agreements, and the recognition of Israel. (6)

As well, the IDF's July 2014 attack was preceded
by another Israeli action in April that further exacerbated
existing tensions. As Moun Rabbani wrote in the *London
Review of Books*, "Negotiations that had been going
on for nine months stalled after the Israeli government
reneged on its commitment to release a number of Palestinian prisoners, incarcerated since before the 1993 Oslo
Accords..." (7) The Netanyahu regime felt it could not risk
being seen as too conciliatory with an election looming,
and again these developments were notably absent in
corporate media coverage of the July, 2014, violence.

There are good reasons why The Israeli state utterly opposes any unification of Palestinian factions.

One is that the Hamas-Fatah conflict has provided a useful pretext for refusing to engage in serious negotiations. How can one negotiate with a divided entity? More significantly, for more than 20 years, Israel has been committed to separating Gaza from the West Bank in violation of the Oslo Accords it signed in 1993, which declare Gaza and the West Bank to be an inseparable territorial unity. (8)

Such unification would seriously interfere with Israeli plans to dominate the West Bank and isolate existing Palestinian enclaves as current maps indicate. These plans bode ill for the shrinking prospects of a viable Palestinian state.

Separated from Gaza, any West Bank enclaves left to Palestinians have no access to the outside world. They are contained by two hostile powers, Israel and Jordan, both close U.S. allies...Furthermore, Israel has been systematically taking over the Jordan Valley, driving out Palestinians, establishing settlements, sinking wells, and otherwise ensuring that the region—about one-third of the West Bank, with much of its arable land—will ultimately be integrated into Israel... (9)

As previously mentioned, the IDF required a pretext for Operation Protective Edge and, "Such an occasion arose when three Israeli boys from the settler community in the West Bank were brutally murdered. The Israeli government evidently quickly realized that they were dead, but pretended otherwise, which provided the opportunity to launch a 'rescue operation' ..." (10) ... and the ensuing invasion of Gaza. The pattern is well-established but unremarked in the pages of publications like the *Globe and Mail* and the *National Post.*

... Bell does offer some excellent insights about the motives of the Irgun and the Stern Gang, which also help to explain why other terrorist groups also perpetrate seemingly hopeless acts of violence. Bell's keenest observation was that the Irgun used violent acts of terrorism because they wanted to force the British to interrogate and imprison members of the Jewish community in Palestine to create more sympathizers and increase support for their terrorist group within the Yishuv. This is an important point because other terrorist groups have also justified their use of violence by saying it is designed to provoke government crackdowns on the general population that will, in turn, create more sympathizers for the terrorist groups within the communities they operate in. (11)

THE SUBJECTIVITY OF TERRORISM: PALESTINIAN VERSUS ISRAELI GUERRILLA TACTICS

While Israeli leaders and Western pundits offer scathing critiques of Hamas "human shield" tactics, a glance backwards reveal Jewish guerrillas operating with similar tactics and motives in the late nineteen-forties:

Similarly, Palestinian terror acts have consistently invited the wrath of the IDF and Israeli state security services that target Gaza Palestinians in retaliatory actions like air raids, artillery attacks and collective punishments like border closings. The Israeli state may well be a vibrant democracy but the Palestinians under Israeli authority are subject to arbitrary arrest and confinement without charge under a harsh penal code designed to break their will to resist occupation and oppression. Israel's prisons are full of Palestinian prisoners with little recourse to comprehensive legal representation. In fairness, occasionally captured Israeli soldiers have fared little better in Palestinian custody and are usually used for prisoner exchange. As well, Palestinian desperation has spawned a martyr's cult of suicide bombers. Ironically, the mass suicide of Jews under Roman attack at Masada is still venerated as a sacred act of nobility.

THE CANADIAN ANGLE

Prime Minister Stephen Harper has presented Canadians with a false choice on Middle East peace: either voice "absolute, non-negotiable belief in Israel" or be declared an anti-Semite. Emma Teitel of Maclean's wrote that, "His cheerleading for the Jewish state was excessive enough (even for a Jew) that it verged on the absurd." (12) Stephen Harper refuses to be a real friend to the Israelis in the sense that he openly excuses their more objectionable behaviour for the sake of political support, fundamentalist religiosity and what he calls principle.

"Two days after Harper won a minority government on January 23, Hamas won Canadian-monitored
and facilitated elections in Palestine." (13) Canada was
quick to condemn these fair and democratic elections
and immediately cut off aid to Gaza. "The aid cutoff,
which was designed to sow division within Palestinian
society, had devastating social effects." (14) Since
Canada is among those few nations (also Israel and the
U.S.) who consider Hamas a terrorist entity, it is worth
commenting on the Harper government's approach to
the highly subjective concept of terrorism.

Much like the corporate media, the vital element
of context is absent from the government's stance
although it is probably aware of the history of Hamas
and the inevitability of its creation. An *Ottawa Citizen*
editorial of September 16, 2014, examined the fact that
Harper refuses to acknowledge or investigate the root
causes of terrorism, choosing instead to simply declare
it an "evil" that must be fought with state security and
military forces. The editorial states that "Conservatives
like to use 'root causes' as code for naive and simplistic
attempts to excuse terrorism as the inevitable result of
poverty or some other social factor."

It is beyond dispute that the magnitude of Jewish
terrorism in pre-1948 Palestine and the current violence
perpetrated by illegal Israeli settlers has been mini-
mized in the Western media. Such violence remains
safely outside the realm of examination. Refusing to
discuss the root causes of any given problem almost
guarantees its perpetuation. To do so for myopic political advantage is, at the very least, reckless.

Prominent among Harper's Canadian supporters is Conservative senator Linda Frum, sister to neoconservative writer David Frum. When asked about Canadian Jewish support for the Harper government, Senator Frum was quoted in *Maclean's* magazine as saying that Canadian Jews had simply grown tired of the "...notion that, when Israelis and Palestinians quarrel, Canada should consider the grievances of both sides equally." (15) In the current climate, Senator Frum can rest easy in that regard. Canada signed the Canada-Israel Free Trade Agreement in 1997 for political and economic reasons. "In an implicit recognition of the occupation, Canada's free trade accord with Israel includes the West Bank as a place where the country's customs laws apply. Canada's trade agreement is based on the areas Israel maintains territorial control over, not on internationally-recognized borders." (16) Considering these facts, it's safe to assume that Canada would have applied the same standard to Israel settlements in Gaza, had the territory not been abandoned. In stark contrast, Engler notes that "The European Union's trade agreement with Israel...explicitly excludes products from territory Israel captured in the 1967 war and occupies against international law."

MEDIA ABUSE OF HOLOCAUST MEMORY IN GAZA COVERAGE

Sun Media columnist Ezra Levant, in a July 28, 2014, *Toronto Sun* article on Gaza and the goals of Hamas, begged this query for rhetorical discussion: "Serious question: If Hamas terrorists in Gaza were to build

Auschwitz-style ovens to burn Jews like the Nazis did, would the world still demand that Israel stop attacking them?" Employing the horror of the Nazi Holocaust is a classic fallacy of reason whereby someone seeks to discredit their opponents by employing a distracting appeal to emotion and guilt. Were Friedrich Nietzsche alive today he might well consider Levant a man who … throw [s] a bit of their personality after their bad arguments, as if that might straighten their paths and turn them into right and good arguments—just as a man in a bowling alley, after he has let go of the ball, still tries to direct it with gestures." (17)

The validity of this observation on Levant's crude tactic highlights the misleading presence of fallacious reasoning on the pages of publications that routinely ignore the conventions of reasoned discourse.

THE EVACUATION OF GAZA'S GUSH KATIF JEWISH SETTLEMENT: INVENTING A NATIONAL TRAUMA

The IDF's July 2005 mass evacuation of over ten thousand Jewish settlers from Gaza's Gush Katif settlement became the subject of a 2010 study by a group of Israeli psychologists called *The Mental Preparation for the Disengagement and Its Aftermath in the IDF*. According to *Brainwashed* author Rachel Ginsberg: "How was the IDF transformed into an army of expulsion, where 40,000 soldiers and 20,000 police were able to carry out with clockwork precision the most morally controversial and painful mission it ever faced, without flinching." (18) Perhaps Ginsberg forgets that there was no need to transform the IDF into an army of expulsion since the force has specialized in mass expulsions of Palestinians since 1948. Beyond that, might she apply the same moral standards to those IDF soldiers who participated in the brutal 2008-09, 2012 and 2104 attacks on Gaza?

It is likely that the Israeli government of 2005 was aware that a mass evacuation of Jewish settlers from Gaza would be very unpopular with IDF soldiers. However, soldiers throughout history have routinely undergone desensitization training to facilitate the completion of unpleasant missions. The evacuation of Gush Katif by all accounts was a peaceful operation although the mass exit from Gaza was stridently opposed by Israeli expansionists determined to create more "facts on the ground."

> Instead of carrying out the operation straightforwardly; as would have been easy enough, the government decided to stage a national trauma... which meant in practice: we cannot abandon an inch of the Palestinian territories that we want to take in violation of international law. This farce played well in the West but was ridiculed by more astute Israeli commentators ... (19)

Unfortunately, Ginsberg's article refers to Gaza's Palestinians only as "the enemy"; a faceless horde to be feared and hated. She actually likens the IDF's Gush Katif evacuation tactics to World War Two Nazism and declares all Israelis the victims of government persecution. I must ask, though, if the IDF can indoctrinate its soldiers to peacefully evacuate Jewish settlements in Gaza, surely they could replicate their efforts in the West Bank and East Jerusalem?

MILITARY DISSENT IN ISRAEL

In spite of vehement condemnations and denials by the Netanyahu government, members of elite IDF military formations, including forty-three members of Intelligence Unit 8200, refused in 2014 to serve in Gaza and the West Bank. Members of this special unit sent a letter to Israeli Prime Minister Benjamin Netanyahu saying they refused to "take part in actions against Palestinians" and "continue serving as tools in cementing the military's control over the Occupied Territories." The letter ... singled out the unit's surveillance of Palestinians and accused it of collecting information that is "used for political persecution" and "harms innocent people." (20) Netanyahu, a former commando and noted militarist, later tempered his harsh criticism of Unit 8200 and praised it along with other elite IDF units. While the military protest movement is still relatively small, there exists a growing consensus, particularly among reservists, that the IDF is harming both its international reputation and morale by using military force to oppress Palestinian civilians.

SOLUTIONS

Nothing significant will happen for the Palestinians until the United States decides to withdraw its military, diplomatic and economic support for Israel: the factors that permit the Jewish state to behave with unjust impunity.

Concerning Canada's role, the Harper government recently announced $66 million in aid to the Palestinian Authority in stark contrast to their former threats to cut all funding if the Palestinian Authority pursued the modest goal of securing observer status at the UN. Rather than donate Canadian tax dollars, Harper would do better by encouraging the Israelis to relinquish control of Gaza's borders, air space and coastal zones, thereby empowering the Palestinians to fully profit from agriculture, fishing, manufacturing, tourism and the extraction of offshore natural gas reserves. The profits from these industries would largely solve Gaza's financial woes and restore dignified independence to her people. Beyond that, a free and secure Gaza would provide a positive example for other groups struggling for peace and autonomy.

1. Do you think a double standard exists regarding media coverage of Israel, in that settlement of occupied territory and other aggressive acts are rarely condemned?

2. How might one organize and advocate for Palestinian autonomy in daily life?

"STATE OF TERROR," BY CHRISTINA PAZZANESE FEATURING JESSICA STERN, FROM *HOOVER DIGEST*, ORIGINALLY PUBLISHED IN THE *HARVARD GAZETTE* JUNE 19, 2015

JESSICA STERN, A MEMBER OF HOOVER'S TASK FORCE ON NATIONAL SECURITY AND LAW, SHOWS HOW ISIS USES A SLICK, MEDIA-SAVVY CAMPAIGN TO LURE VULNERABLE YOUTH TO ITS END-TIMES ARMY

Family and friends describe them not as radicals but as well-behaved, diligent students at a private high school in London. So it came as a shock when the three British girls slipped their passports into handbags, casually walked out of their homes, and boarded a flight to Istanbul to join the Islamic State, or ISIS, in Syria. British authorities believe that the teenagers, who disappeared in February, were probably aided by Aqsa Mahmood, a young woman originally from Scotland who recruits for the extremist group.

The young women's highly publicized defection to Syria, as well as the arrest of three young British men in Istanbul as they headed to join ISIS in March, are among the latest cases of teenagers and young adults from middle-class, educated, often suburban backgrounds in Britain, the United States, Canada, and various European nations who have been enticed to abandon their comfortable lives and join the Islamic State. In late February, the Washington Post identified "Jihadi John," the masked man seen in several ISIS videos beheading hostages, as a college-educated computer programmer from a well-off family in West London. James Clapper, director of US national intelligence, told Congress earlier this year that an estimated 3,400 citizens from Western countries have traveled to Iraq and Syria, presumably to join ISIS.

Jessica Stern serves on the Hoover Institution's Jean Perkins Task Force on National Security and Law and was a member of the National Security Council staff during the Clinton administration. She is also fellow at the FXB Center for Health and Human Rights at the Harvard T.H. Chan School of Public Health and a lecturer in government at Harvard. Stern has written extensively about terrorism and violent extremists. Her latest book is *ISIS: The State of Terror*, co-written with J. M. Berger. Stern spoke with the *Gazette* about how and why ISIS has succeeded at luring young Westerners to its side.

Christina Pazzanese, Harvard Gazette: We know that the so-called Islamic State is extraordinarily media-savvy. What social media platforms have been most effective in reaching Western recruits?

Jessica Stern: There's been a lot of activity on Twitter. Aqsa Mahmood is a good example. She's been accused of enticing the three young women from London who apparently left their homes to join the Islamic State. She's also known as Umm Layth, which means "mother of the lion." She spoke to them on Twitter, and then they ended up moving to an encrypted platform to continue their discussion, which is a common recruitment tactic. [Mahmood] also answers questions on ask.fm. Somehow her postings are attracting young women, some of them very high-achieving, to leave home to join the jihad.

There's a big debate about what should be taken off Twitter and whether Twitter is inadvertently facilitating terrorist recruitment. Twitter's automated list of "who to follow" makes it easy for a person interested in ISIS to rapidly find additional ISIS supporters. Sometimes, ISIS accounts are suspended, but often, shortly afterward, a new account with a new name appears, which serious followers can find.

There's a debate among those who think we should allow those accounts to remain active and those who think that Twitter should be suspending terrorist accounts. Those who say that the accounts should be left alone argue that they're a good way to gather intelligence, and that removing them would only result in recruiters moving to a less-transparent platform. Those who want the accounts shut down say that private companies should not allow ISIS and other groups to use social media to recruit followers, and that terrorists' use of social media to promote violence does not constitute protected speech. Twitter recently suspended over two thousand ISIS-related accounts. ISIS has now declared war against Twitter, threatening the lives of its staff.

Pazzanese: What is the pitch to male and female potential recruits?

Stern: For the men, it's "Come and fight if you can fight; if you can't fight we also need doctors, we need social-media experts, engineers.... We're running a state, and so if you feel you can't handle fighting, we can still use you." The women are often recruited to marry jihadists: "You can participate in the jihad by marrying. You can be the mother of the next generation." It is a fairly traditional female role. There are tremendous social benefits for recruits: you're making the world a better place, or so the group claims, which provides a kind of spiritual reward. There's financial reward for the fighters. ISIS actually pays the fighters, gives them free housing, offers to provide them wives. Hence, the need to recruit young women. There's also the tremendous lure of extreme fundamentalism. I think we can all understand the appeal: wouldn't it be nice to have easy answers to every morally complex question? Inside a group like ISIS, life becomes morally simple. The rules are clear. Good and evil come out in stark relief.

IN SEARCH OF LOST YOUTH

Pazzanese: What's the psychological profile of those people most susceptible to their message?

Stern: We don't have a profile of the Westerners joining ISIS yet because there haven't been large studies. But I can tell you that [British intelligence agency] MI5 did a study of Westerners who were involved in or closely associated with extremist activity, prior to ISIS's recent recruitment drive. They found that a surprisingly high number of them were converts to Islam. Many in the MI5 study were relatively ignorant of Islam, even if they were Muslim. Umm Layth is a good example. She grew up in a secular Muslim family and went from relative ignorance about Islam to recruiting for ISIS.

An important factor seems to be the desire to forge a new identity, an identity with dignity. I interviewed terrorists for many years and I can tell you that identity is often absolutely key. We also know that there is a higher rate of mental illness among so-called lone wolves, people who are inspired (often online) to commit terrorist actions without physically joining an extremist group. Studies of Westerners joining jihadi organizations, prior to ISIS's recruitment drive, have shown that foreign fighters tend to be alienated or marginalized within their own societies; they may have had a bad encounter with police or distrust local authorities. They tend to disapprove of their nation's foreign policies. If they're living in an ethnic enclave, they're likely to be alienated from people living alongside them, as well as the country as a whole, whether it's the United States or the UK or elsewhere in the West. For those who join ISIS, I think that there's got to be an element of thrill-seeking as well, perhaps even an attraction to violence. It's hard for me to imagine that anybody who gets recruited today doesn't know about ISIS's extreme brutality.

Pazzanese: Is the impulse to join the Islamic State very different from, say, the idealistic impulse of young people to join the Peace Corps or a nongovernmental organization, or any global organization they believe is doing important and uplifting work?

Stern: Many of the people who join terrorist organizations believe they are making the world a better place. They see pictures of [Syrian leader Bashar] al-Assad's brutality against his own people and they feel the desire to help. That sense of righteousness is a very appealing aspect of joining a terrorist group, for some. But I would say in some ways it's more like joining the Weather Underground than the Peace Corps. At this point, it's hard to imagine anyone joining without knowing that they're going to be involved in real atrocities.

Pazzanese: But in their minds, those actions are righteous.

Stern: Absolutely.

Pazzanese: How effective is Mahmood as a recruiter, and what makes these Western recruiters so successful? Do they tend to be true believers or mere cynical mercenaries?

Stern: She is very effective. My guess is that it's partly because she knows how to relate to young women like herself. She knows their lives. ISIS is using Westerners to run the social media campaign to recruit Westerners.

Pazzanese: The State Department has recently announced that it has stepped up its countermessaging efforts. What are they doing, and is that likely to be sufficient, given the sophisticated and prolific nature of the Islamic State?

Stern: They have a program called "Think Again Turn Away," and if you look at what they've been doing and compare it with what ISIS has been doing, it's so boring. ISIS has professional cameramen . . .

Pazzanese: The ISIS production values are quite high. It's not like the old Al-Qaeda training videos we used to see.

Stern: No, it's not. If you look at what the State Department puts out, sadly, you can tell that they didn't have a lot of money. But the guy who ran that program told me, "Look, I know we can't compete with the video imagery showing, 'Here's your chance to create this very pure state, and you're going to get to kill infidels and Shiites.' "

Pazzanese: They can't compete on the messaging or on the production values?

Stern: Both. ISIS has made an enemy of the entire world, other than those who join it. I hope that we're going to get much more serious—we outside the government—to find ways to respond. There is a program that I'd like to bring to Harvard. I've been advocating for years to have young people design countermessaging programs, rather than State Department employees or Madison Avenue. There is an organization, EdVenture Partners, that created a curriculum for students around the world to compete to create the most effective countermessaging. The students will create digital platforms to amplify the messages of clerics who can argue against ISIS's interpretation of Islam, or of former members of ISIS who turned against the organization. Those are just two examples; there are all kinds of things that can be done. The initiative is called "P2P: Challenging Extremism." I would love to get students from across the university, students in engineering, students in political science, students who speak languages, or who are very good at communication....

ideally we want a completely interdisciplinary group. I'm just so excited about this.

Pazzanese: Besides better coordinating the State Department's fragmented messaging efforts, I wonder if that's ever going to be sufficient compared to the prolific nature of ISIS. I understand they're sending out as many as two hundred thousand social media messages per day.

Stern: No. It's never going to be enough. I think the private sector has to get involved.

ISIS'S END GAME—LITERALLY

Pazzanese: What is the Islamic State's endgame? Is it to provoke global Armageddon, or does it want to control the world and have everyone live under its terms?

Stern: They want to establish a worldwide caliphate. The dream is to take over the world. They are also obsessed with the Apocalypse. Although ISIS claims to justify its actions by referring to religious texts, ordinary Muslims have no idea what ISIS is talking about. The Quran is not an apocalyptic book, so ISIS has to borrow from different apocalyptic narratives. Their online English-language magazine is called *Dabiq*, which is the name of the town where ISIS believes the final battle of the Apocalypse will take place.

They believe that sexually enslaving women who are from religious minorities is a good thing; it's a sign that the end times are coming. They also justify sexual slavery as a way of avoiding the sin of adultery or premarital sex, because if you have sex with a slave, it's not really sex, or so they claim. They can be pedophiles.

Pazzanese: Why is religion such a useful framework or pretext for terrorism, subjugation, and genocide?
Stern: ISIS is a millenarian movement. They want to create a new human being the same way the Soviets wanted to create a new human being. They want to re-create humanity and they want to create a purified world. It's a cosmic battle to them. It's not totally different from communism or other ideologies, but God is a pretty compelling citation.

Pazzanese: Does religion give it a patina of righteousness or defuse any accusations that this is a mere power grab?

Stern: I think religion is often a patina or marketing strategy for terrorists to accomplish more worldly goals. In the case of ISIS, many of the leaders are former Baathists, the secular political party that ruled Iraq prior to the 2003 invasion. [Abu Bakr] al-Baghdadi, the "caliph" of the Islamic State, recruited former military and intelligence personnel from Saddam Hussein's Iraq. They have important, useful skills. ISIS's religious agenda is clearly intermingled with its more secular goals. ISIS is capitalizing on the feeling among Sunni Muslims that they are under threat in the new Iraq, and that ISIS is the only protection they have from the Iraqi leadership's anti-Sunni, sectarian policies.

Pazzanese: In human history, where does ISIS rank in terms of what they've been able to accomplish—their lethality and their organizational strength—in such a brief amount of time?

Stern: Compared with modern terrorist organizations that we know, they rank very high. However, compared with the Khmer Rouge, the Nazis, the communists, they rank pretty low both in terms of their accomplishments and even in terms of their brutality. We've seen much worse. ISIS is not just a terrorist group; it is also an insurgent army. While it's shocking to see how much territory ISIS acquired so quickly, we're comparing it with terrorist groups that weren't necessarily trying to acquire large amounts of territory. The ideology, the brutality of this group—I have to think they're going to self-destruct before they manage to spread as far as, say, the communists or the Nazis. The Nazis weren't advertising their atrocities; ISIS is publicizing its atrocities, flaunting its brutality. It's part of the end-times narrative that ISIS hopes to spin.

1. Should Twitter and other social media companies suspend accounts suspected of being operated by ISIS? Or is it better to keep tabs on them on a public platform?

2. If you were asked to design a media countermessaging campaign against ISIS recruitment tactics, what message of theirs would you focus on debunking, and how?

"TWO VIEWS: THE U.S. AND RUSSIA IN SYRIA," BY PATRICK J. BUCHANAN, FROM THE *WASHINGTON REPORT ON MIDDLE EAST AFFAIRS*, NOVEMBER/DECEMBER 2015

WAR PARTY TARGETS PUTIN AND ASSAD

Having established a base on the Syrian coast, Vladimir Putin on Sept. 30 began air strikes on ISIS and other rebel forces seeking to overthrow Bashar Assad.

A longtime ally of Syria, Russia wants to preserve its toehold on the Mediterranean, help Assad repel the threat, and keep the Islamic terrorists out of Damascus.

Russia is also fearful that the fall of Assad would free up the Chechen terrorists in Syria to return to Russia.

In intervening to save Assad, Putin is doing exactly what we are doing to save our imperiled allies in Baghdad and Kabul.

Yet Putin's intervention has ignited an almost berserk reaction.

John McCain has called for sending the Free Syrian Army surface-to-air missiles to bring down Russian planes. Not only could this lead to a U.S.-Russia clash, but U.S.-backed Syrian rebels have a record of transferring weapons to the al-Qaeda affiliate.

The end result of McCain's initiative, sending Stingers to Syria, could be airliners blown out of the sky across the Middle East.

Hillary Clinton wants the U.S. to create a no-fly zone. And the Oct. 2 *Wall Street Journal* endorsed the idea:

"Mr. Obama could make Mr. Putin pay a price.... In Syria the U.S. could set up a no-fly zone to create a safe haven for refugees against ... Mr. Assad's barrel bombs. He could say U.S. planes will fly wherever they want, and if one is attacked the U.S. will respond in kind."

U.S.-Russian dogfights over Syria are just fine with the Journal.

On Oct. 3 *The Washington Post* seconded the motion, admonishing Obama: "Carve out safe zones. Destroy the helicopter fleet Mr. Assad uses for his war crimes."

Has the War Party thought this through?

Establishing a no-fly zone over Syria, which means shooting down Syrian fighter-bombers and helicopters, is an act of war. But when did Congress authorize the president to go to war with Syria?

When last Obama requested such authority—in 2013, when chemical weapons were used—the American people arose as one to say no to U.S. intervention. Congress backed away without even voting.

Unprovoked air strikes on Syrian government forces would represent an unauthorized and unconstitutional American war. Does the Party of the Constitution no longer care about the Constitution?

Is a Republican Congress really willing to give Barack Obama a blank check to take us to war with Syria, should he choose to do so?

Is this what America voted for in 2014?

A no-fly zone means U.S. warplanes downing Syrian planes and helicopters and bombing anti-aircraft defenses at Syrian airfields.

To Damascus this would mean the Americans have committed to the defeat of their armed forces and downfall of their regime.

The Syrians would fight—and not only the Syrian army. For Russia, Hezbollah and Iran are all allied to the Damascus regime, as all believe they have a vital interest in its survival.

How would Russia, Iran and Hezbollah respond to U.S. air strikes on their ally? Would they pack it in and leave? Is that our experience with these folks?

Today, the U.S. is conducting strikes on ISIS, and the al-Qaeda affiliate. But if we begin to attack the Syrian army or air force, we will be in a new war where the entire Shi'i Crescent of Iran, Baghdad, Damascus and Hezbollah, backed by Russia, will be on the other side.

We will have taken the Sunni side in the Sunni-Shi'i sectarian long war.

How long such a war would last, and how it would end, no one knows.

Whatever one thinks of Putin's policy in Syria, at least it makes sense. He is supporting an ally, the Assad regime, against its enemies, who seek to overthrow that regime.

It is U.S. policy in Syria that makes no sense.

We train rebels at immense cost to fight Assad who cannot or will not fight. We attack ISIS, which also seeks to bring down the Assad regime. And we, too, want to bring down Assad.

Who do we think will rise if Assad falls?

Do we have a "government in a box" that we think we can fly to Damascus and put into power if the Syrian army collapses, the regime falls and ISIS approaches the capital?

Have we forgotten the lesson of *Animal Farm*? When the animals revolt and take over the farm, the pigs wind up in charge.

For months, Sen. Tim Kaine of Virginia has called on Congress to debate and decide before we launch any new war in the Middle East.

One wishes him well. For it is obvious that the same blockheads who told us that if the Taliban and Saddam and Qaddafi fell, liberal democracy would arise and flourish, are now clamoring for another American war in Syria to bring down Assad.

And who says stay out? Donald Trump and Bernie Sanders, both of whom also opposed the U.S. invasion of Iraq.

There is something to be said for outsiders.

Patrick J. Buchanan is the author of the new book The Greatest Comeback: How Richard Nixon Rose From Defeat to Create the New Majority. *Copyright © 2015 Creators Syndicate, Inc. Reprinted by permission of Patrick J. Buchanan and Creators Syndicate, Inc.*

SHOULD U.S. ALLY WITH AL-QAEDA IN SYRIA?

BY ROBERT PARRY

The key sentence in *The New York Times'* Sept. 30 lead article about Russian airstrikes against Syrian rebel targets fell to the bottom of the story, five paragraphs from the end, where the *Times* noted in passing that the area north of Homs where the attacks occurred had been the site of an offensive by a coalition "including Nusra Front."

What the *Times* didn't say in that context was that Nusra Front is al-Qaeda's affiliate in Syria, an omission perhaps explained because this additional information would disrupt the righteous tone of the article, accusing Russia of bad faith in attacking rebel groups other than the Islamic State.

But the Russians had made clear their intent was to engage in airstrikes against the *mélange* of rebel groups in which al-Qaeda as well as the Islamic State played prominent roles. *The Times* and the rest of the mainstream U.S. media are just playing games when they pretend otherwise.

Plus, the reality about Syria's splintered rebel coalition is that it is virtually impossible to distinguish between the few "moderate" rebels and the many Sunni extremists. Indeed, many "moderates," including some trained and armed by the CIA and Pentagon, have joined with al-Qaeda's Nusra Front, even turning over U.S. weapons and equipment to this affiliate of the terrorist organization that attacked New York and Washington on Sept. 11, 2001. Lest we forget, it was that event that prompted the direct U.S. military intervention in the Middle East.

However, in recent months, the Israeli government and its American neoconservative allies have been floating trial balloons regarding whether al-Qaeda could be repackaged as Sunni "moderates" and become a *de facto* U.S. ally in achieving a "regime change" in Syria, ousting President Bashar al-Assad, who has been near the top of the Israeli/neocon hit list for years.

A key neocon propaganda theme has been to spin the conspiracy theory that Assad and the Islamic State are somehow in cahoots and thus al-Qaeda represents the lesser evil. Though there is no evidence to support this conspiracy theory, it was even raised by Charlie Rose in his "60 Minutes" interview Sept. 27 with Russian President Vladimir Putin. The reality is that the Islamic State and al-Qaeda have both been leading the fight to destroy the secular Assad government, which has fought back against both groups.

And, if these two leading terror groups saw a chance to raise their black flags over Damascus, they might well mend their tactical rifts. They would have much to gain by overthrowing Assad's regime, which is the principal protector of Syria's Christians, Alawites, Shi'i and other "heretics."

The primary dispute between al-Qaeda and the Islamic State, which began as "al-Qaeda in Iraq," is when to start a fundamentalist caliphate. The Islamic State believes the caliphate can begin now, while al-Qaeda says the priority should be mounting more terrorist attacks against the West.

Yet, if Damascus falls, the two groups could both get a measure of satisfaction: the Islamic State could busy itself beheadings the "heretics" while al-Qaeda could plot dramatic new terror attacks against Western targets, a grim win-win.

One might think that the U.S. government should focus on averting such an eventuality, but the hysterical anti-Russian bias of *The New York Times* and the rest of the mainstream media means that whatever Putin does must be cast in the most negative light.

THE ANTI-PUTIN FRENZY

On Oct. 1, one CNN anchor ranted about Putin's air force attacking "our guys," i.e., CIA-trained rebels, and demanded to know what could be done to stop the Russian attacks. This frenzy was fed by the *Times'* article, co-written by neocon national security correspondent Michael R. Gordon, a leading promoter of the Iraq-WMD scam in 2002.

The *Times* article pushed the theme that Russians were attacking the white-hatted "moderate" rebels in violation of Russia's supposed commitment to fight the Islamic State only. But Putin never restricted his military support for the Assad government to attacks on the Islamic State.

Indeed, even the *Times* began that part of the story by citing Putin's quote that Russia was acting "preventatively to fight and destroy militants and terrorists on the territories that they already occupied." Putin did not limit Russia's actions to the Islamic State. But the Times article acts as if the phrase "militants and terrorists" could only apply to the Islamic State, writing: "But American officials said the attack was not directed at the Islamic State but at other opposition groups fighting against the [Syrian] government."

Unless *The New York Times* no longer believes that al-Qaeda is a terrorist group, the Times' phrasing doesn't make sense. Indeed, al-Qaeda's Nusra Front has emerged as the lead element of the so-called Army of Conquest, a coalition of rebel forces which has been using sophisticated U.S. weaponry including TOW missiles to achieve major advances against the Syrian military around the city of Idlib. The weaponry most likely comes from U.S. regional allies, since Saudi Arabia, Turkey, Qatar and other Sunni-led Gulf states have been supporting al-Qaeda, the Islamic State and other Sunni rebel groups in Syria. This reality was disclosed in a Defense Intelligence Agency report and was blurted out by Vice President Joe Biden.

On Oct. 2, 2014, Biden told an audience at Harvard's Kennedy School: "our allies in the region were our largest problem in Syria ... the Saudis, the emirates, etc., what were they doing? They were so determined to take down Assad and essentially have a proxy Sunni-Shi'i war, what did they do? They poured hundreds of millions of dollars and tens of thousands of tons of military weapons into anyone who would fight against Assad, except the people who were being supplied were Al Nusra and al-Qaeda and the extremist elements of *jihadis* coming from other parts of the world."

Al-Qaeda's Nusra Front also has benefited from a *de facto* alliance with Israel which has taken in wounded Nusra fighters for medical treatment and then returned them to the battlefield around the Golan Heights. Israel also has carried out airstrikes inside Syria in support of Nusra's advances, including killing Hezbollah and Iranian advisers helping the Syrian government.

The Israeli airstrikes inside Syria, like those conducted by the United States and its allies, are in violation of international law because they do not have the permission of the Syrian government, but those Israeli and U.S. coalition attacks are treated as right and proper by the mainstream U.S. media in contrast to the Russian airstrikes, which are treated as illicit even though they are carried out at the invitation of Syria's recognized government.

OBAMA'S CHOICE

Ultimately, President Barack Obama will have to decide if he wants to cooperate with Russia and Iran in beating back al-Qaeda, the Islamic State and other *jihadists*—or realign U.S. policy in accord with Israel's obsession with "regime change" in Syria, even if that means a victory by al-Qaeda. In other words, should the United States come full circle in the Middle East and help al-Qaeda win?

Preferring al-Qaeda over Assad is the Israeli position—embraced by many neocons, too. The priority for the Israeli/neocon strategy has been to seek "regime change" in Syria as a way to counter Iran and its support for Lebanon's Hezbollah, both part of Shi'i Islam.

According to this thinking, if Assad, an Alawite, a branch of Shi'i Islam, can be removed, a new Sunni-dominated regime in Syria would disrupt Hezbollah's supply lines from Iran and thus free up Israel to act more aggressively against both the Palestinians and Iran.

For instance, if Israel decides to crack down again on the Palestinians or bomb Iran's nuclear sites, it now has to worry about Hezbollah in southern Lebanon raining down missiles on major Israeli cities. However, if Hezbollah's source of Iranian missiles gets blocked by a new Sunni regime in Damascus, the worry of Hezbollah attacks would be lessened.

Israel's preference for al-Qaeda over Assad has been acknowledged by senior Israeli officials for the past two years, though never noted in the U.S. mainstream media. In September 2013, Israel's Ambassador to the United States Michael Oren, then a close adviser to Israeli Prime Minister Binyamin Netanyahu, told the Jerusalem Post that Israel favored the Sunni extremists over Assad.

"The greatest danger to Israel is by the strategic arc that extends from Tehran, to Damascus to Beirut. And we saw the Assad regime as the keystone in that arc," Oren told the Jerusalem Post in an interview. "We always wanted Bashar Assad to go, we always preferred the bad guys who weren't backed by Iran to the bad guys who were backed by Iran." He said this was the case even if the "bad guys" were affiliated with al-Qaeda.

And, in June 2014, then speaking as a former ambassador at an Aspen Institute conference, Oren expanded on his position, saying Israel would even prefer a victory by the brutal Islamic State over continuation of the Iranian-backed Assad in Syria. "From Israel's perspective, if there's got to be an evil that's got to prevail, let the Sunni evil prevail," Oren said. [See Consortiumnews.com's "Al-Qaeda, Saudi Arabia and Israel."]

So, that is the choice facing President Obama and the American people. Despite the misleading reporting by *The New York Times*, CNN and other major U.S. news outlets, the realistic options are quite stark: either work with Russia, Iran and the Syrian military to beat back the Sunni *jihadists* in Syria (while seeking a power-sharing arrangement in Damascus that includes Assad and some of his U.S.-backed political rivals)—or take the side of al-Qaeda and other Sunni extremists, including the Islamic State, with the goal of removing Assad and hoping that the mythical "moderate" rebels might finally materialize and somehow wrest control of Damascus.

Though I'm told that Obama privately has made the first choice, he is so fearful of the political reaction from neocons and their "liberal interventionist" pals that he feels he must act like a tough guy, ridiculing Putin and denouncing Assad.

The danger from this duplicitous approach is that Obama's penchant for talking out of multiple sides of his mouth might end up touching off a confrontation between nuclear-armed America and nuclear-armed Russia, a crisis that his verbal trickery might not be able to control.

1. The American media has a tendency to vilify foreign "bad guys" when we want regime change (think Qaddafi, Saddam Hussein, etc.) Now in Syria we are faced with a situation of multiple bad guys on all sides (Putin, Assad, ISIS)—do you think our desire to simplify conflicts has impeded action in Syria? If so, how? If not, which side should we take, and why?

2. Is the claim that nuclear confrontation with Russia could result from former president Obama's penchant for taking multiple sides of an issue credible?

CHAPTER 6

WHAT ORDINARY PEOPLE SAY

After protracted war in Iraq and Afghanistan—operations that most experts agree have contributed more to destabilizing the region than any advancing of US interests—it is perhaps unsurprising that Americans have opposed militarized conflict in the Middle East during Obama's presidency. However, that tide might be slowly turning. Polling now shows that a majority of Americans support military action against the Islamic State in Iraq and Syria, albeit in a limited capacity.

With the emergence of such a clear villain as ISIS onto the international stage, one might also expect Americans to support full-scale efforts to take out this dangerous and well-funded insurgent terrorist group. Yet, few are calling for anything more than "surgical" air strikes. Have we learned our lesson that inflicting massive damage is not a viable long-term strategy to foster lasting stability in the region?

Not likely. A few auxiliary factors account more for America's comparatively judicious use of force in recent years. As Matt Baum points out in the interview below, gas prices have been low, and barring a few "lone wolf" shooters, there has not been a significant attack on American soil since 9/11. This accounts for a relative lack of public knowledge and engagement, which in turn increases media and official influence over popular opinion, and gives the president more latitude to pursue actions that are politically expedient.

That could change very quickly. A large-scale terrorist action in America would very likely sway public opinion back towards an invasion—one in which no one can foresee a positive resolution.

"AIR STRIKES AGAINST THE ISLAMIC STATE (ISIS): PUBLIC OPINION AND HISTORICAL PERSPECTIVE," BY LEIGHTON WALTER KILLE, FROM *JOURNALIST'S RESOURCE*, SEPTEMBER 23, 2014

[Editor's note: Charts are not included in this text.]

Facing what it perceived as a growing threat from the Islamic State (ISIS), a large insurgent group that has taken over parts of Syria and Iraq, the Obama administration has begun air strikes targeting its forces, including, for the first time, on

Syrian soil. Recent polls — for example, by Washington Post-ABC News and Wall Street Journal/NBC News — have suggested significant public support for this effort. This support stands in apparent contrast to the results of some polling in summer 2014, which suggested continuing opposition to any military operations abroad. Such data had prompted observers to characterize Americans as increasingly war-weary and more isolationist, following more than a decade of conflict in Iraq and Afghanistan.

Any swing toward supporting military action could represent an important shift in public opinion. But this apparent shift also comes despite the fact that, according to Gallup, Americans have increasingly seen terrorism as less of a pressing priority over the past decade; and a majority continue to say that the country should not have invaded Iraq in 2003 and should not conduct direct military action again to support the Iraqi government in its fight against the Islamic State. Past opinion polls have also shown that the U.S. public has been consistently wary about military intervention in the Syrian civil war, even as chemical weapons were used by the regime in 2013 and as the country's refugee crisis has grown to historic proportions.

At this point it remains unclear if American public opinion is changing more generally on military and foreign policy issues, or if recent shifts are unique to the challenge posed by the Islamic State. After all, public sentiment is often unpredictable on matters of war and peace, as history shows. How does the current sentiment of Americans compare with public sentiment on the eve of — or at key turning points during — prior conflicts?

The following are snapshots of U.S. public opinion about the country's participation in conflicts across the past 60 years — from the Korean War to the air campaign in Libya — through the lens of Gallup polls. The questions asked by Gallup are not always parallel between separate polls, but the patterns and responses nevertheless furnish interesting and useful historical perspective.

MARCH 2011: ENFORCING THE U.N. "NO FLY" ZONE IN LIBYA

In a March 21 poll conducted after the United States joined other countries in conducting air strikes against Muammar Qaddafi's forces to enforce the United Nations' no-fly zone, 47% of respondents approved U.S. actions, while 37% did not. While more respondents agreed than disagreed, the levels of support were lower than those for earlier U.S. military campaigns, including Iraq in 2003 (76% for, 20% against), Afghanistan in 2001 after the World Trade Center attacks (90% for, 5% against), and Afghanistan and the Sudan in 1998 (66% versus 19%). Prior to Libya, the U.S. military interventions that received the lowest public approvals were Kosovo and the Balkans in 1999 (51% for, 45% against), Haiti in 1994 (54% for, 45% against) and Grenada in 1983 (53% versus 35%).

NOVEMBER 2009: THE AFGHANISTAN TROOP "SURGE"

From November 20 to 22, 2009, Gallup conducted a poll on public support for four options in the ongoing Afghanistan conflict: The first was to increase the number of U.S. troops by the approximately 40,000 — commonly referred to as the "surge" — the option recommended by the U.S.

commanding general at the time. The other options were to increase troop levels but by a smaller amount; keep the number of troops the same; or begin to reduce the number of soldiers. A plurality of the respondents, 39%, wanted to reduce troop levels, while 37% supported a "surge." Only 10% supported a smaller increase in troop levels, and 9% wanted to keep them the same. On November 30, President Obama ordered 30,000 additional troops to Afghanistan.

MARCH 2003: 48 HOURS FOR SADDAM HUSSEIN TO LEAVE IRAQ

On November 8, 2002, the United Nations passed a resolution stating that Iraq was in "material breach" of the ceasefire terms agreed to after the Persian Gulf war in 1991. After the 2002 vote, three months of warnings by the United States, debate by the U.N. and rhetoric from Iraqi officials followed, until U.S. President George W. Bush announced that the U.S. would attack unless Hussein left the country within 48 hours. For Iraqis, the possibility of war was suddenly very real. Gallup asked 783 U.S. residents their opinions on Bush's decision: 66% approved, while 30% disapproved.

OCTOBER 2001: MILITARY INTERVENTION IN AFGHANISTAN AFTER 9/11

Precisely one month after the attacks on the World Trade Center and Pentagon, nearly 500 U.S. residents were asked if they favored or opposed "direct military action" by the United States in Afghanistan. Just over 88% approved the United States taking such action, while 10% opposed, and the remainder either didn't know or declined to answer.

In the same poll, a plurality of the respondents, 47%, said that the most important problem facing the country was terrorism; the economy in general was the second-most important problem (13%).

OCTOBER 1998: AIR STRIKES AGAINST SERBIAN FORCES IN KOSOVO

After a massacre of ethnic Albanians in Kosovo was attributed to Serbian forces, a divided U.N. Security Council held an emergency meeting after passing an earlier measure authorizing the use of military force. In the United States, more than a thousand respondents were asked whether the U.S. and its European allies should conduct air strikes against the Serbian forces in Kosovo. The response was closely divided: Just under 42% said that they approved military action, while 41% did not. The remainder, 17.25%, didn't know or declined to answer.

FEBRUARY 1994: ETHNIC AND RELIGIOUS CONFLICT IN BOSNIA

On February 5, 1994, a crowded marketplace in Sarajevo was targeted by mortar-fire during the four-year-old siege of the city. Nearly 70 people died and hundreds more were injured. A poll conducted on the following Monday, a subset of U.S. residents were asked "Would you rather see the Muslims win or the Serbians win, or are you not sure?" Of those who responded, just 10% favored either one, while the vast majority of respondents either didn't know (81%) or didn't answer (9%). Opinions were almost precisely split on President Clinton's handling of the crisis — 37% approved and 37% disapproved — while the balance weren't sure.

MAY 1993: U.S. TROOPS TO BOSNIA?

As the ethic and religious conflicts in Bosnia steadily worsened after the 1992 breakup of the former Yugoslavia, there were calls for the United States to send troops to the country. Just three years earlier the United States had rapidly bested Saddam Hussein's troops after the invasion of Kuwait, yet the ghosts of earlier, far bloodier conflicts of U.S. troops remained. The question asked was: "If the United States were to send troops to Bosnia, do you think that situation would end up being more like the Vietnam War or more like the Persian Gulf War?" Just under half of respondents (49%) felt it would be relatively rapid, while 43% thought it had the potential of turning into a military quagmire.

DECEMBER 1990: THE IRAQI INVASION AND OCCUPATION OF KUWAIT

After months of rhetoric, accusations and troop movements by Saddam Hussein, Iraq invaded Kuwait in August 1990 and proclaimed the country to be its 19th province. There were fears over the potential for the conflict widening to neighboring Saudi Arabia, a strong ally of the United States and the country's largest supplier of petroleum. Nearly 1,700 respondents were asked how closely they followed news about the situation and whether the Mideast situation was worth going to war over. Nearly half (49%) said it was worth fighting a war, while 44% said it wasn't. In the same poll, the performance of president George H.W. Bush was favored by respondents at a two-to-one ratio, with 63% expressing approval and 30% disapproval.

MARCH 1986: LIBYA FIRES MISSILES AT U.S. PLANES AND THE AIR FORCE RESPONDS

In 1973 Libyan leader Muammar Qaddafi stated that Libya had exclusive rights to the entire Gulf of Sidra, in the center of the country's coastline; the U.S. asserted that international law applied, and in early 1986 held maneuvers in the gulf. On March 23 conflict broke out: Libya fired several missiles and the U.S. replied in force, taking out ground radar installations as well as a Libyan boat. A U.S. poll held afterward asked: "Do you feel U.S. attacks against Libyan ships and military sites were justified or not?" Nearly three-quarters of the respondents said the attacks were justified, while 15% said they weren't.

FEBRUARY 1965: THE U.S. CONFLICT BEGINS TO ESCALATE IN VIETNAM

In August 1964 the U.S. Congress passed the Gulf of Tonkin Resolution, which gave President Lyndon B. Johnson the power to conduct military operations in Southeast Asia without a declaration of war. In February 1965, six months later, Gallup asked more than 3,500 poll participants if the United States should continue its efforts in Vietnam, even at the risk of nuclear war. More than 40% approved, saying the U.S. should continue, while 34% disapproved. Nearly 70% of respondents approved of President Johnson's handling of his job as president, while 18% disapproved. Vietnam was seen as the country's biggest problem by 29% of those polled, while 25% saw civil rights as the most important issue.

JULY 1950: NORTH KOREA INVADES SOUTH KOREA

Just five years after the end of World War II, North Korea invaded its southern neighbor in June 1950. A month after, Gallup asked 1,236 U.S. residents the following questions: "Do you think the Communists in China will send soldiers to help the North Koreans fight against U.S. and allied troops, or not? If they do, do you think the United States should go to war against Communist China, or not?" More than half (54%) said the U.S. should go to war with China if the country sent troops to help the North Koreans; 27% said it shouldn't, while 19% had no opinion.

For those interested in historical public opinion research, the Gallup Brain website is a rich resource. It contains the results of a wide range of polls conducted since the Gallup organization's founding in 1935.

1. What patterns emerge as we look at public opinion on US engagement historically?

2. How does your opinion regarding these armed conflicts compare to the Americans surveyed?

"INTERVENTION IN SYRIA, THE MEDIA, AND PUBLIC OPINION: RESEARCH CHAT WITH HARVARD'S MATT BAUM," BY JOHN WIHBEY, FROM *JOURNALIST'S RESOURCE,* AUGUST 27, 2013

Matthew A. Baum is the Kalb Professor of Global Communications at the Harvard Kennedy School. His research focuses on the intersection of domestic politics, international conflict and American foreign policy, as well as on the role of the news media and public opinion in contemporary American politics. His 2010 book *War Stories: The Causes and Consequences of Public Views of War,* co-authored with UCLA's Tim J. Groeling, is a comprehensive examination of issues such as media story framing and the effects on public sentiment.

Baum's 2013 study "The Iraq Coalition of the *Willing and (Politically) Able:* Party Systems, the Press, and Public Influence on Foreign Policy," published in the *American Journal of Political Science*, furnishes a number of insights relevant to the current moment, as American and international intervention is being contemplated in the Syrian conflict. He demonstrates the key role the news media can play in decisions of war and peace. "In an era of rapidly expanding and diversifying media," Baum writes, "the potential for media to influence foreign policy via its effects on citizen awareness of and attitudes regarding the activities of their leaders is ... increasing."

As part of our ongoing "research chat" series, we asked him about intervention in Syria and what we might learn from examining public deliberation and media coverage on the eve of prior conflicts. The following is an edited interview:

Journalist's Resource: Based on the historical evidence, what do we know about the interplay between American public opinion and the President's decision to go to war or intervene in a modern conflict? What is relevant to consider with respect to Syria?

Matt Baum: There are several important things to keep in mind. The first is the degree to which the public is engaged with the issue, and that can be due to factors having nothing to do with the administration's policy preferences. Engagement can also be a function of the overt effort by the administration to gain public interest in the policy — and acquiescence perhaps — or to keep the public distracted so it can have a relatively free hand. I think it's safe to say that a President would like as free a hand as possible in foreign policy, and a lot of scrutiny reduces his latitude. All else equal — and it's rarely equal — a President would prefer not to spend a lot of time talking about an impending conflict. But there are factors weighing against that. The President might think that if you can draw a line in the sand, you might send a credible signal to the guy you are contemplating going to war against that you mean business. This might cause them to back down. As we know in hindsight, there has been more than one occasion when our adversaries didn't really believe we were going to do what we said we were going to do. That's not always true. Some-times adversaries are willing to accept that risk, but there are times when they really didn't believe it.

When George H.W. Bush went public on Iraq's August 1990 invasion of Kuwait and loudly proclaimed "This will not stand," he tied his own hands and basically put himself in a position where he really couldn't back down — and sent a clear signal to Saddam Hussein, who, we have since learned, didn't really believe it. This is different than 2003 and the Iraq War, when Hussein believed he could hold out long enough that the coalition would fracture. So there are these variables: When do you want to get the public engaged, and when do you not? It's interesting that we've had so much conflict in the past decade or so that it's actually more difficult than it was to get the public really focused. The long conflict in Iraq was of intense interest domestically for a very extended period. It sort of sucked the oxygen out of any potential public engagement with Afghanistan, giving President Obama a relatively free hand there, for better or worse. He was never under that much political pres-sure there.

The next instance was Libya, where there was very little risk to American lives. It was an air campaign. The administration didn't talk about it much and the American public didn't pay much attention. In Syria, where a conflict has been dragging on for several years, we're in a situa-tion where our economy is somewhat less dependent on the comings and goings of crises in the Middle East. We've had several years of the Arab Spring — the upheavals of the Middle East — and gas prices have not changed that much. I think there's not all that much interest.

JR: Which brings us to today, and potential intervention in Syria. What does this all add up to in terms of understanding the public and policymakers now?

Matt Baum: I think that the fact that the polls say Americans are wary in Syria does not mean all that much. If the Obama administration is able to do something that has a decisive effect, they will look like heroes. And if they look impotent in their use of military force, it will rebound against them. But the polling numbers showing American reticence, as of right now, doesn't add up to much, because it's really not a salient issue. It's not enough to look at the numbers of people opposing intervention; you have to look at how much people care and at this point it isn't very high on the list, as of today. That can change if things escalate and it starts to look like a "real" war, as opposed to Libya — which was obviously real if you were there — but from the United States the perspective was that no Americans were on the ground and no American planes were being shot down. If Syria looks like that, the public won't get all that engaged. It would potentially be a foreign policy success for the Obama administration, though coming awfully late, after a lot of horrible things have happened there. But if it doesn't go well and America is gradually sucked in — throwing good resources after bad — eventually it could become a big political liability, and you could get significant public engagement. This could have happened in Afghanistan, too, if more Americans started getting killed. But it hasn't escalated in that way.

JR: Let's talk about the press and mass media effects on the public. There were obviously lots of criticisms

about the way the press covered the run-up to the
Iraq War. What are some lessons to bear in mind for
the press?

Matt Baum: As far as I can tell, if you look at the New
York Times, Washington Post or Wall Street Journal you
are seeing the right questions. There is a lot more skepticism now than, say, the run-up to the Iraq War. During
2002-2003, critical thinking was out there in the press,
but it was overwhelmed by the Bush administration's
all-out effort to justify its conflict. Here, with Syria, you
have an intervention that, by all accounts, will not be
anything like that scale and neither is the public relations campaign. I interpret that to mean that the Obama
administration wants to do what it needs to do to get
enough support and pursue its policies — but not even
a little bit more. That's all it wants to do. Because the
last thing the administration needs is intense scrutiny
of its actions there. I don't think it believes it's going to
get Syrian President Assad to back down and surrender the keys to the palace because of whatever threats
it might make. That neutralizes the benefits of drawing
lines in the sand for the Obama administration.

Overall, I guess that I'm not that critical in terms of
how journalists have been covering Syria in that regard.

JR: Sometimes there is a narrative logic that devel-
ops in foreign policy stories, where there is a bad
guy and the whole goal is to get rid of him and there
is not much consideration of what comes next. This
can lead to a failure to think through the post-con-
flict, or post-regime, consequences and environment.

Matt Baum: The press, in its effort to be neutral, usually focuses on process and strategy and not on geopolitical ramifications. Reporters tend to look at decisions — who is making them and when — and they don't ask the "So what?" questions. As soon as you get into them, it becomes tough to appear objective — they're going to lead you to normative conclusions. Let's say you explore the idea that intervention could lead to fragmentation, deterioration and ultimately the unraveling of the state of Syria. That could be disastrous. If you write a story that says that, that has a normative implication, whether you intend it or not. There is a tendency, at least within the legacy media, not to do that sort of thing, or at least not emphasize it.

Then there is the fact that there are not that many reporters who have a particularly deep understanding of the Middle East. There aren't that many Americans who have deep knowledge of the region — myself included. So it would be really hard for very many journalists — maybe Tom Friedman and a few others can do this in a sophisticated way — to play out the long-term geopolitical implications in an appropriate way. Rather than putting yourself out on a ledge, it makes more sense if you are a reporter to talk about process and strategy — what the decisions are and what's happening, not the implications of what is being done. That's a much heavier lift.

There's a lot of evidence suggesting that journalists' coverage tends to reflect the tenor of elite debate in Washington. Right now, on the Syria question, it appears that among Congressional leaders, the serious foreign policy centers and others, opinion is sort of all over the map. Several prominent Republicans who support military action — Senators McCain and Graham and the like — say we should intervene, though no boots on the ground. Libertarian types adamantly oppose it. Democrats are always betwixt and between on aggressive use of force, because they tend to not like them based on principle. But their guy, President Obama, is in power. They are pushed and pulled.

So this is a case that maximizes the ability of the media to influence public opinion, because there is not a clear narrative coming out of Washington. When there is a clear narrative and elites are pretty much lined up, that is going to be the story. It's like trying to swim in quicksand to go against it as a reporter. With Syria, this is the opposite: This is a case where you can find any story line you want and find prominent supporters for it. Those are the cases when the press can really have influence on public opinion — and they may well have with Syria. It is very different than Iraq in 2003, for instance, in that regard.

JR: How does the fact there was, very likely, a major chemical weapons attack on civilians in Syria change the dynamics and the calculus around public opinion and presidential decision-making?

Matt Baum: The President drew that line on weapons of mass destruction, and now the administration is likely saying, "Darn, I wish we had not drawn that line in the sand." I suspect they don't really want to use force in Syria; I suspect they don't think they have great options there. But the line was drawn very publicly, and so now as the provocations get more and more overt — and it gets harder and harder to obfuscate about whether the Syrian government really did use such weapons — the Obama administration is kind of backed into a corner. It works to their advantage in terms of the contextual buildup and framing around weapons of mass destruction. The message is that it's the Rubicon that one cannot cross, and woe be it to anyone who crosses the Rubicon. We've heard this ever since the Gulf War pretty much non-stop, mostly with respect to Iraq but not always. So there is a very salient, accessible narrative there for the press to latch on to and the public to grasp and accept. If you cross that line, you are going to be punished. I think that explains why you've got some Republicans supporting military action, as much as anything. Without the chemical weapons in the equation, I don't think you'd be talking about direct engagement in Syria. It would be much less likely. I don't think the strategic environment has changed that much. We don't really have anyone to support who we have that much confidence in. There is no liberal Democrat. The rebels aren't the "moral equivalent of our Founding Fathers," as President Ronald Reagan called the Contras in Nicaragua.

JR: For deeper perspective, is there any academic work, beyond your own book *War Stories*, that might be a relevant read on these questions of war and the public?

Matt Baum: I would recommend reading: American Public Opinion on the Iraq War, by Ole Holsti; John Mueller's "The Iraq Syndrome," in *Foreign Affairs*; and the book *Taken by Storm: The Media, Public Opinion and U.S. Foreign Policy in the Gulf War.*

1. How much influence does the media have on your feelings about US military engagement overseas?

2. Do you think former president Obama made a mistake by declaring a "red line" with chemical weapons?

"RAND PAUL AND THE MYTH OF AMERICAN ISOLATIONISM," BY PETER BEINART, FROM THE *NATIONAL JOURNAL*, OCTOBER 17, 2014

In an op-ed last year in The Washington Post, former Sens. Joe Lieberman and Jon Kyl warned of "the danger of repeating the cycle of American isolationism." That summer, Post columnist Charles Krauthammer heralded "the return of the most venerable strain of conservative foreign policy: isolationism." New York Times columnist Bill Keller then fretted that "America is again in a deep isolationist mood." This November, Wall Street Journal columnist Bret Stephens will publish a book subtitled The New Isolationism and the Coming Global Disorder.

What makes these warnings odd is that in contemporary foreign policy discourse, isolationism—as the dictionary defines it—does not exist. Calling your opponent an "isolationist" serves the same function in foreign policy that calling her a "socialist" serves in domestic policy. While the term itself is nebulous, it evokes a frightening past, and thus vilifies opposing arguments without actually rebutting them. For hawks eager to discredit any serious critique of America's military interventions in the "war on terror," that's very useful indeed.

TO GRASP HOW little basis today's attacks on "isolationism" have in reality, it's worth understanding what the term "isolationism" actually means. Merriam-Webster defines it as "the belief that a country should not be involved with other countries." The Oxford dictionaries call it "a policy of remaining apart from the affairs or interests of ... other countries."

When critics decry isolationism today, they usually map that dictionary definition onto a particular historical period: the 1920s and 1930s. Warnings about isolationism almost always come with the same historical morality tale: America turned inward in the interwar years, and the world went to hell. That's what makes "isolationism" scary. Like "socialism," it's a euphemism for "Hitler and Stalin are coming."

The problem is that isolationism—as commonly understood—not only doesn't fit American foreign policy today, it doesn't even fit American foreign policy in the 1920s and 1930s. There are plenty of valid critiques of how the United States comported itself on the world stage between World War I and World War II. But the claim that America detached itself from other countries is simply not true. In 1921, for instance, President Harding summoned the world's powers to the Washington Naval Conference

and pushed through what some have called the first disar-
mament treaty in history. In 1924, after Germany's failure to
pay its war reparations led French and Belgian troops to
occupy the Ruhr Valley, the Coolidge administration ended
the crisis by appointing banker Charles Dawes to design
a new reparations-payments system, which Washington
muscled the European powers into accepting. American
pressure helped to produce the 1925 Treaty of Locarno,
which guaranteed the borders between Germany and
the countries to its west (though not, fatefully, to its
east). In 1930, President Hoover played a key role in the
London Naval Conference, which placed further limits on
naval construction.

Dr. Seuss drew many anti-isolationism cartoons
during the early 1940s. Again and again during the interwar
years, the U.S. deployed its newfound economic power
to shape politics in Europe. And this overseas engagement wasn't limited to America's government alone.
Although the United States severely limited European
immigration in the 1920s, Americans built the avowedly
internationalist institutions that would help guide the
country's foreign policy after World War II. The Council
on Foreign Relations was born in 1921. The University
of Chicago created America's first graduate program
in international affairs in 1928. And during the interwar
years, American travel to Europe expanded dramat-
ically. To be sure, the U.S. in the interwar years was
more comfortable intervening economically and diplomatically than militarily. But despite the Neutrality Acts
meant to keep the U.S. out of another European war, the
Roosevelt administration began sending warplanes and
warships to Britain two years before Pearl Harbor. By

early 1941, long before America officially entered the war, its ships were already hunting German vessels across the Atlantic.

The only sense in which the United States in the interwar years truly remained apart from other nations lay in its refusal to make binding military commitments, either via the League of Nations or through alliances with particular nations. America wielded power economically, diplomatically, and even militarily, but it jealously guarded its sovereignty. That's why one influential history of the era dubs U.S. foreign policy between the wars "independent internationalism." (The last prominent spokesperson for that form of independence was Sen. Robert Taft of Ohio, who during the early Cold War opposed NATO because it required that America pledge itself to Europe's defense, but who endorsed an all-out war with China to reunify Korea under Western control.) The popular "characterization of America as isolationist in the interwar period," argues Ohio State University's Bear Braumoeller in a useful review of the academic literature on the period, "is simply wrong."

If calling America isolationist in the 1920s and 1930s is wrong, calling America isolationist today is absurd. The United States currently stations troops in more than 150 countries. Its alliances commit it to defend large swaths of Europe and Asia against foreign attack. Recent presidents have dropped bombs on, or sent troops to, Kuwait, Iraq, Afghanistan, Bosnia, Kosovo, Somalia, Sudan, Syria, Libya, Pakistan, and Yemen. Last month, President Obama sent 3,000 American troops to battle an Ebola outbreak in West Africa. And while Americans fiercely debate particular military interventions and foreign-aid programs, the general presumption that the United States should play a leading role in solving problems far from our shores is largely uncontested in the American political mainstream.

Just how uncontested becomes clear when you examine the foreign policy evolution of Rand Paul, the man frequently held up as the leader of his party's isolationist wing. As a Senate candidate in 2009, Paul mused about reducing America's military bases overseas. In 2011, soon after entering the Senate, he suggested eliminating foreign aid. He has also repeatedly insisted that only Congress, and not the president, can declare war (a position that Barack Obama championed when he was in the Senate as well).

Even these views did not make Paul an isolationist. He has never questioned America's membership in NATO, for instance, or its security alliance with Japan, the cornerstones of America's post-World War II global role. But in Paul's early days on the national political stage, his foreign policy instincts did diverge substantially from the ones that held sway in official Washington.

What has happened since shows just how hegemonic America's globalist consensus actually is.

For starters, Paul's efforts to dial back American interventionism went nowhere. His Senate bill to end foreign aid to Egypt, Pakistan, and Libya got 10 votes. A later bid to reduce America's overall aid budget from $30 billion to $5 billion garnered 18 votes. This at a time when, according to Bill Keller, America was in "a deep isolationist mood."

Moreover, Paul's own views have become markedly more conventional. After first saying that the U.S. should not "tweak Russia for its aggression in Ukraine,

Paul later called for imposing harsh sanctions on Moscow, reinstalling missile-defense systems in Poland and the Czech Republic, and boycotting the Winter Olympics in Sochi. On ISIS, Paul has followed a similar path. After expressing initial skepticism about the value of air strikes, he now says "If I had been in President Obama's shoes, I would have acted more decisively and strongly against ISIS."

Were Paul really an isolationist, his approach to the Middle East would be straightforward: Extricate America from the region and stop giving its people reasons to hate us. But he has explicitly repudiated that view. "I don't agree that absent Western occupation, that radical Islam goes quietly into that good night, " he said in a speech last year. "Radical Islam is no fleeting fad but a relentless force." Paul has even attacked Obama for "disengaging diplomatically in Iraq and the region."

Instead, over the last year, Paul has developed an approach patterned on the internationalist thinking that influenced foreign policy elites during the Cold War. In a speech last February, Paul said the United States should contain jihadist Islam the way George Kennan envisioned containing Soviet Communism. For Kennan, containment represented an alternative to both isolationism and war. It required buttressing partners that could halt the expansion of Soviet power without trying to roll it back, since that would risk war. Whether one can usefully transfer the concept of containment to the current "war on terror" is questionable. But in invoking Kennan, Paul was expressing a preference for steady, cautious, long-term American engagement in the Middle East—hardly what you'd expect from an isolationist.

Besides containment, Paul's other watchword is "stability." "What much of the foreign policy elite fails to grasp is that intervention to topple secular dictators has been the prime source of that chaos," he said last month "From Hussein to Assad to Qaddafi, we have the same history. Intervention topples the secular dictator. Chaos ensues, and radical jihadists emerge. ... Intervention that destabilizes the region is a mistake."

Against both liberal interventionists and "neoconservatives" who support intervention to produce more democratic, pro-Western regimes, in other words, Paul wants the United States to support the Arab world's traditional, comparatively secular autocrats, because at least they keep the region under control. His core argument with hawks such as John McCain and Lindsey Graham is not over whether America should withdraw from the Middle East. It's over whether America should use its influence there to prop up the old order or usher in something new. That's why Paul now peppers his speeches with quotes from Colin Powell, Robert Gates, and Dick Cheney circa 1991, policymakers who cut their teeth in the more risk-averse but still undoubtedly internationalist Republican Party of Henry Kissingerand George H.W. Bush. As Jason Zengerle recently pointed out in The New Republic, Paul's foreign policy has become a fairly standard brand of realism, with some anxiety over unchecked presidential power thrown in.

Critics see this as cynical. Paul, as numerous articles have noted, has grown more hawkish as he's courted the donors he needs to fund his likely presidential campaign. But the fact that Paul is, by necessity, drawing closer to a foreign policy consensus he once challenged is evidence not of that consensus's weakness, but of its strength.

THAT CONSENSUS WITHIN the political class is not built upon big-dollar donations alone. There are certainly differences between how party elites want the United States to behave around the world and what ordinary citizens desire. But contrary to much media commentary, isolationism is not only largely absent from foreign policy discourse in Washington. It's also largely absent from foreign policy discourse among the public at large.

Last December, a poll by the Pew Research Center found that, by 52 percent to 38 percent, Americans wanted the U.S. to "mind its own business internationally," the largest gap in a half-century. The poll sparked a torrent of journalistic anxiety. "American isolationism," fretted a Washington Post headline "just hit a 50-year high."

But upon closer examination, it becomes clear that Americans don't actually want their country to "mind its own business" overseas at all. The same Pew poll that supposedly revealed Americans to be isolationists also found that, by a margin of more than 40 percentage points, they believe that "greater U.S. involvement in the global economy is a good thing." Fifty-six percent of respondents told Pew the United States should "cooperate fully with the United Nations." Seventy-seven percent agreed that, "in deciding on its foreign policies, the U.S. should take into account the views of its major allies." And a clear majority opposed the idea that "since the U.S. is the most powerful nation in the world, we should go our own way in international matters." In that same vein, a recent study by the Chicago Council on Global Affairs found that 59 percent of Americans want the U.S. to maintain its overseas military deployments at current levels. It also found that when told how much the U.S. spends on defense and foreign aid, Americans urge cutting the former but want the latter to go up.

How can a public that endorses greater economic globalization, far-flung military bases, extensive coordination with American allies and the United Nations, and higher foreign aid also say it wants the U.S. to "mind its own business" internationally? The answer lies in the way Washington elites have defined America's international "business." In recent years, America's highest-profile overseas behavior has been its military interventions, either directly or via proxies, in Afghanistan, Iraq, Libya, Syria, and, at one point, potentially Ukraine. When Pew conducted its poll in late 2013, it was those interventions that Americans rejected, not international engagement, or even military action, per se.

The Chicago Council poll teased out the distinction. Like Pew, it uncovered an ostensibly high level of isolationism: Forty-one percent of respondents said it would "be best for the future of the country" if "we stay out of world affairs." But when the council dug deeper, it found "Even those who say the United States should stay out of world affairs would support sending U.S. troops to combat terrorism and Iran's nuclear program. However, many of the conflicts in the press today—for example, in Syria and Ukraine—are not seen by the public as vital threats to the United States." It's no surprise, therefore, that since September, when the ISIS beheadings convinced many Americans that the chaos in Iraq and Syria might threaten them, the percentage supporting military action in those countries has shot up.

In important ways, in fact, the standard claim that elites must overcome the ingrained isolationism of ordinary Americans gets things backward. When it comes to working through the U.N. or paying heed to America's allies, the public is more sympathetic to international cooperation than are many Beltway insiders. In official Washington, for instance, it is virtually taken for granted that America must remain the world's lone superpower. By contrast, ordinary Americans, according to Pew overwhelmingly want America to play a "shared leadership role" with other countries. Only 12 percent want America to be the "single world leader," the same percentage who want America to play "no leadership role" at all.

GIVEN THE OVERWHELMING evidence, both from politicians and the public, that isolationism in America today is virtually nonexistent, why do so many high-profile commentators and politicians depict it as a grave threat? One clue lies in a word that these Cassandras use as a virtual synonym for isolationism: "retreat." If the subtitle of Bret Stephens's forthcoming book is The New Isolationism and the Coming Global Disorder, its title is America in Retreat. In their op-ed warning of a new "cycle of American isolationism," Lieberman and Kyl employ variations of "retreat" or "retrench" six times.

But "isolationism" and "retreat" are entirely different things. Isolationism has a fixed meaning: avoiding contact with other nations. Retreat, by contrast, only gains meaning relatively. The mere fact that a country is retreating tells you nothing about the extent of its interactions overseas. You need to know the position it is retreating from.

Herein lies the rub. In general, the isolationism-slayers are far more comfortable bemoaning American retreat than defending the military frontiers from which America is retreating. That's because those frontiers, which reached their apex under George W. Bush, were both historically unprecedented and historically calamitous.

To realize how historically unprecedented they were, it's worth remembering how much more circumscribed America's military ambitions were under Ronald Reagan. He could not have imagined sending ground troops to invade Afghanistan or Iraq. For one thing, both countries were clients of the Soviet Union. For another, the bitter legacy of Vietnam made sending hundreds of thousands of troops to overthrow a government half a world away inconceivable. During his eight years in office, Reagan invaded only one foreign country: Grenada, whose army boasted 600 troops. In his final year in the White House, when some administration hawks suggested he invade Panama, Reagan adamantly refused. The idea struck him as far too risky.

Equally inconceivable was the idea of deploying American troops on former Soviet soil. One of the disputes that initially led hawks to label Rand Paul an isolationist was the Kentuckian's 2011 opposition to admitting the former Soviet republic of Georgia into NATO, an issue that put him in conflict with fellow GOP rising star Marco Rubio. But if Paul is an isolationist because he opposes an American military guarantee to defend Georgia, what does that make James Baker, who in 1990 reportedly promised Mikhail Gorbachev that if Moscow allowed Germany to reunify, NATO would not expand "one inch" further east:

not even into East Germany, let alone the rest of Eastern Europe, let alone the former Soviet Union itself.

Between Reagan's presidency and Obama's, America's military frontier advanced to fill the gap left by the collapse of Soviet power. Aspects of that expansion turned out well. George H.W. Bush reestablished Kuwait's sovereignty in the first Persian Gulf War; Bill Clinton helped stabilize southeastern Europe by waging war to stop Slobodan Milosevic's rampage through Bosnia and later Kosovo; countries such as Poland, Hungary, and the Czech Republic have prospered under NATO protection.

But in Afghanistan and Iraq, America's forward march turned catastrophic. More than twice as many Americans have died in those two wars than in the September 11 attacks that justified them. A 2013 study by Linda J. Bilmes of Harvard's Kennedy School of Government estimates that they will ultimately cost the United States between $4 trillion and $6 trillion. As a result, she argues, their financial legacy "will dominate future federal budgets for decades to come."

Obama has made mistakes in his retreat from those wars. (I've been particularly critical of him for disengaging diplomatically from Iraq while Nuri al-Maliki was pushing his country's Sunnis into the arms of ISIS.) But the notion that Obama should not have retreated—that he should have defended a historically unprecedented military frontier in wars that were causing America debilitating long-term fiscal damage and snuffing out thousands of young American lives, against insurgencies that posed no direct or imminent threat to the United States—is hard to forthrightly defend. Which is why hawks rarely defend it. Instead, they equate retreat with isolationism and isolationism with a fictionalized account of the 1920s and 1930s. And, presto, Obama becomes a latter-day Neville Chamberlain while they become heirs to Winston Churchill rather than to a guy named Bush.

Hawks worried that Barack Obama, or Rand Paul, or the American people have not defended American interests forcefully enough in Iraq, Syria, Ukraine, or Iran can make plenty of legitimate arguments. Calling their opponents "isolationists" isn't one of them. It's time journalists greet that slur with the same derision they currently reserve for epithets like "socialist," "fascist," and "totalitarian." Then, perhaps, we can have the foreign policy debate America deserves.

1. Why does the author state that American hasn't really been isolationist in the past 100 years?

2. What do you think about the policy of isolationism, as the author sets out here? Do you think America should adopt more isolationist policies?

CONCLUSION

The US invasion of Iraq failed to bring lasting democratic rule to the nation. Americans began to see Iraqi occupation as costly and futile, putting pressure on former president Obama to withdraw. This coincided with ramped-up sectarian violence in the country. Meanwhile, the Arab Spring's high hopes for democratic reform in the Middle East also ended in temporary setback. Beginning in Tunisia in 2010, young people organized to demand less income inequality, more job opportunities, and reform of corrupt autocratic regimes. Rather than give concessions, dictators such as president Bashar al-Assad in Syria began to crack down on populations with extreme violence. This has led to civil war and a massive refugee crisis, exacerbating regional tensions and international

These two developments brought chaos and confusion to the Middle East, leaving a vast power vacuum as well—the perfect storm for ISIS to step into. Although ISIS has caused few American deaths to date, their commitment to worldwide terror could conceivably provoke future ground wars, depending on the mood and leadership of the country.

For the time being however, expert and public opinion alike see few credible options for US intervention due to a lack of trustworthy allies, increased energy independence, and an overall shift in attention from the Middle East to Asia. Whether this becomes a stable paradigm shift or just a temporary reprieve remains to be seen.

The US invasion of Iraq failed to bring lasting demo-cratic rule to the nation. Americans began to see Iraqi occupation as costly and futile, putting pressure on for-mer president Obama to withdraw. This coincided with ramped-up sectarian violence in the country. Meanwhile, the Arab Spring's high hopes for democratic reform in the Middle East also ended in temporary setback. Beginning in Tunisia in 2010, young people organized to demand less income inequality, more job opportunities, and reform of corrupt autocratic regimes. Rather than give conces-sions, dictators such as president Bashar al-Assad in Syria began to crack down on populations with extreme violence. This has led to civil war and a massive refugee crisis, exacerbating regional tensions and international

These two developments brought chaos and confu-sion to the Middle East, leaving a vast power vacuum as well—the perfect storm for ISIS to step into. Although ISIS has caused few American deaths to date, their commitment to worldwide terror could conceivably provoke future ground wars, depending on the mood and leadership of the country.

For the time being however, expert and public opinion alike see few credible options for US intervention due to a lack of trustworthy allies, increased energy independence, and an overall shift in attention from the Middle East to Asia. Whether this becomes a stable paradigm shift or just a temporary reprieve remains to be seen.

ABOUT THE EDITOR

Anne Cunningham has a PhD in Comparative Literature, and has published articles on women modernist writers and feminist theory. She currently works as an Instructor of English at the University of New Mexico—Taos. She is also a songwriter and performer, and lives with her husband and music partner David Lerner in Arroyo Hondo, NM.

BIBLIOGRAPHY

Babbin, Jed. "Obama's Drone War,"*The American Spectator*, May 2013. (http://spectator.org/55756_obamas-drone-war).

Baum, Matthew, And John Wihbey. "Intervention In Syria, The News Media And Public Opinion: Research Chat With Harvard's Matt Baum." *Journalist's Resource*, August 27, 2013. (http://journalistsresource.org/tip-sheets/research/syria-intervention-public-opinion-research-chat-harvard-matt-baum).

Beinart, Peter. "Rand Paul and the Myth of American Isolationism." *National Journal*, October 17, 2014. (http://www.defense-one.com/politics/2014/10/rand-paul-and-myth-american-isolationism/96875).

Biden, Joseph R., Jr. "Breathing Room: Stepping Back To Move Forward In Iraq." *The National Interest*, 85, 2006. pp.36-40.

Broder, Jonathan. "Gambling On Iran: The Nuclear Deal And The Legacy Of John Kerry," *Newsweek*, July 31, 2015. (http://www.newsweek.com/2015/08/21/john-kerry-iran-nuclear-deal-358546.html).

Carpenter, Ted Galen. "How The Mideast Was Lost: Neither Dictatorship Nor Democracy Guarantees America's Interests." *The American Conservative*, January 2, 2012 (http://www.theamericanconservative.com/articles/how-the-mideast-was-lost).

Carter, Ashton. "Statement on U.S. Policy and Strategy in the Middle East before the House Armed Services Committee." *US Department of Defense Speeches*, June 17, 2015. (http://www.defense.gov/News/Speeches/Speech-View/Article/606680/statement-on-us-policy-and-strategy-in-the-middle-east-before-the-house-armed-s).

Duchesney, Morgan. "Gaza's Agony: An Alternative Perspective On Recent Events." *Humanist Perspectives* 192 (2015). (http://www.humanistperspectives.org/issue192/duchesney.html).

French, David. "How Our Overly Restrictive Rules of Engagement Keep Us from Winning Wars." *National Review*, December 21, 2015.

Heller, Stanley. "The Left's False Logic On Syria." *Socialist Worker,* March 1, 2016. (https://socialistworker.org/2016/03/01/the-lefts-false-logic-on-syria).

Kane, Tim. "The Good Country." *Commentary*, December 1, 2014 (https://www.commentarymagazine.com/articles/the-good-country).

Katulis, Brian, Lang, Hardin, and Singh, Vikram. "Defeating ISIS: An Integrated Strategy to Advance Middle East Stability." *Center For American Progress*, September 10, 2014. (https://www.americanprogress.org/issues/security/report/2014/09/10/96739/defeating-isis-an-integrated-strategy-to-advance-middle-east-stability/).

Kauffman, Richard A. "A Violent Sorting Out: Middle East Expert Joshua Landis." *The Christian Century*, April 30, 2015 (http://www.christiancentury.org/article/2015-04/violent-sorting-out).

Kille, Leighton Walter. "Air Strikes Against The Islamic State (ISIS): Public Opinion And Historical Perspective." *Journalist's Resource*, September 23, 2014. (http://journalistsresource.org/studies/government/security-military/public-opinion-military-intervention-syria-gallup-polling).

O'Hanlon, Michael. "Deconstructing the Syria Nightmare." *The National Interest*, October 22, 2015 (http://nationalinterest.org/feature/deconstructing-the-syria-nightmare-14108).

Pazzanese, Christina. "State Of Terror." *Hoover Digest*, June 19, 2015. (http://www.hoover.org/research/state-terror).

Podhoretz, John. "The Emergency." *Commentary*, April 1, 2015. (https://www.commentarymagazine.com/articles/the-emergency-1).

CHAPTER NOTES

CHAPTER 5: WHAT THE MEDIA SAY

"GAZA'S AGONY: AN ALTERNATIVE PERSPECTIVE ON RECENT EVENTS," BY MORGAN DUCHESNEY

(1.) Chomsky, Noam & Ilan Pappe: 2010. *Gaza in Crisis.* Chicago: Haymarket Books.

(2.) Rabbani, Mouin: Israel Mows the Lawn in *London Review of Books* 36(15):8; 31 July, 2014.

(3.) Chomsky and Pappe, 2010.

(4.) *Ibid.*

(5.) Chomsky, Noam. Gaza: The Fate of the Ceasefire in www.Tom-Dispatch.ca, September 9, 2014.

(6.) *Ibid*.

(7.) Rabbani, 2014.

(8.) Chomsky, 2014.

(9.) *Ibid.*

(10.) *Ibid.*

(11.) Laffiteau, Charles. Jewish Terrorism and the Creation of the State of Israel, www.academia. edu: August 1, 2014. The work cited is: J.B. Bell, *Terror out of Zion*. New York. St. Martin's Press. 1977.

(12.) Teitel Emma. A friendship with few benefits. *Maclean's*, January 22, 2014.

(13.) Engler, Yves. *The Ugly Canadian*. Vancouver: Red Publishing and Black Point (NS): Fernwood Publishing. 2012.

(14.) *Ibid*.

(15.) Taylor-Vaisey, Nick. Israel's best friend: Stephen Harper. *Maclean's*, December 4, 2013.

(16.) Engler, 2012.

(17.) Kaufmann, Walter. *Basic Writings of Nietzsche: 2000.* Toronto: Random House of Canada.

(18.) Ginsberg, Rachel: *Brainwashed?* in *Mishpacha: Jewish family Weekly*. July 21, 2010.

(19.) Chomsky, Noam. A Middle-East peace that could happen (but won't). In Washington-Speak, "Palestinian State" means "Fried Chicken" *Tom Dispatch*, April 27, 2010. www.tomdispatch.ca

(20.) *Ottawa Citizen*, September 15, 2014.

GLOSSARY

Alawite A sect of Shi'ite Islam in Syria. Most other Muslims view adherents as heretics. Embattled Syrian president Bashar al-Assad and his inner circle belong to this group.

Al-Nusra Front A Sunni Islamist group fighting the Assad government in Syria. This group is closely tied to Al-Qaeda, the group responsible for the September 11 attacks.

Baath Translates as "renaissance"; a pan-Arabist nationalist movement.

Gaza Strip The contested Palestinian territory on the Mediterranean Coast. Israel has withdrawn from Gaza, but many settlers still occupy the land.

Hamas Palestinian Sunni fundamentalist group formed in 1987. Although they are responsible for many terrorist acts, much of Hamas's operating budget also goes to humanitarian efforts aiding Palestinians.

Hezbollah A political party and Shi'a militant group based in Lebanon.

hijab The head-scarf that women must usually wear in public in Islamic societies.

Israeli Defense Force (IDF) The military forces of the state of Israel.

Islamic State in Iraq and the Levant (ISIL) Acronym for the Islamic State in Iraq and Levant, which is a highly militarized quasi-state and terrorist organization in Iraq and Syria; also referred to as the Islamic State (IS) and the Islamic State in Iraq and Syria (ISIS).

jihad A term for a religious duty to improve through struggle. It now means "holy war" in common parlance.

Kurds An ethnic and linguistic Muslim minority group in Iraq, Turkey, and Iran. The United States now views the Kurds as the best of all possible allies against the Islamic State.

Likud A right-wing Israeli political coalition.

mujahideen An Arabic term for one engaged in jihad.

Palestine Liberation Organization (PLO) This group was founded in 1964 with the goal of liberating Palestinians through armed struggle. Its most famous leader was Yasser Arafat.

West Bank The west bank of the Jordan River, captured by Israel in 1967.

FOR MORE INFORMATION

BOOKS

Anderson, Scott. *Lawrence in Arabia: War, Deceit, Imperial Folly and the Making of the Modern Middle East.* New York: Random House, 2014.

Bacevich, Andrew. *America's War for the Greater Middle East: A Military History*. New York: Random House, 2016.

Cambanis, Thanassis *Once Upon a Revolution: An Egyptian Story*. New York: Simon & Schuster, 2015.

Engal, Richard. *And Then All Hell Broke Loose: Two Decades in the Middle East.* New York: Simon & Schuster, 2016.

McHugo, John. *Syria: A History of the Last Hundred Years.* New York: New Press, 2015

Melamed, Avi. *Inside the Middle East: Making Sense of the Most Dangerous and Complicated Region on Earth.* New York: Skyhorse Publishing, 2016.

Pelham, Nicolas. Holy Lands: *Reviving Pluralism in the Middle East.* New York: Columbia Global Reports, 2016

Power, Carla. *If the Oceans Were Ink: An Unlikely Friendship and a Journey to the Heart of the Quran*. New York: Henry Holt, 2015.

Rogan, Eugene. *The Fall of the Ottomans: The Great War in the Middle East.* New York: Perseus, 2015.

Tolan, Sandy. *Children of the Stone: The Power of Music in a Hard Land*. New York: Bloomsbury, 2015.

WEBSITES

Informed Comment

www.juancole.com

Informed Comment is the brainchild of Juan Cole, who is the Richard P. Mitchell Collegiate Professor of History at the University of Michigan. According to his site's description, Cole "has sought to put the relationship of the West and the Muslim world in historical context."

Global Connections: Middle East

www.pbs.org/wgbh/globalconnections/index.html

This site is designed for teachers and features resources from Harvard and UCLA. It also boasts a clean layout, and nice interactive design with geographical tools.

INDEX